RV Passive Income Guide

*Learn to Earn while living in a Motorhome
to become a Real Digital Nomad.*

*Do Your Job and Business in Total Freedom
Traveling and Camping Full Time
With no Worries.*

Written By

Contents

Peter Miller

Hey there folks! I'm Peter Miller, a modern Nomad and businessman that lives full time in an RV.

I was born in 1975, in the Big Sky country, Montana. I was raised in a traditional family, which have been horse herders for generations. Being in contact with nature since childhood, I started experiencing a passion for camping and trekking, making my parents proud of me.

Under the advice of a professor I loved, I undertook marketing studies and I started my brand new working career. After years of being cooped up in the office, I realized that that kind of job and life weren't suitable for me.

While I was living this boring life, I started to feel a certain sense of dissatisfaction and incompleteness, which turned into a desire for freedom.

All at once, making a gut decision and finally buying a caravan from a small dealer in my town, I quitted my job, took my stuff and left.

After spending a lot of time on the road, loving this kind of life, I was still unsatisfied.

I perceived that something important was missing in my life: a job without constraints that could give me stability while experiencing my freedom.

I had various experiences and met millions of other enthusiasts like myself, I tried many jobs and had multiple ideas.

Now, as a marketing expert, I have started several online businesses which have led me this far. All these things made me want to teach others what I learned over the years with my personal experience, easing their way .

"There is no greater joy than knowing that my years of sacrifice will help some other enterprising adventurer like me."

Lastly, I hope my story can make you think about reinventing yourself and gather up the courage to change your life.

HI READER!

I hope you will enjoy this book as much as I enjoyed writing it.

I would love for you to share your opinion with others,
maybe leaving a review!

Every single review is very important to me because it allows me to:

Find out what's missing in my book, updating it for my readers
&
Continue my writing activity

TO BRING YOU NEW HIGH QUALITY CONTENT!

Other people like you may decide to start a revolution in their lives by following the amazing lifestyle *I adopted myself years ago.*

I Thank You for Choosing this Book
&
Wish You a Good Read!

AN IMPORTANT GIFT FOR YOU!

For You who chose this book to *Begin Your RV Adventure,*

WE ARE GIVING AWAY the second book

in the *RV LIFE* collection:

"RV Living for Beginners"

Learn how to <u>live like a true RVer</u>

365 Days a Year

Traveling and Discovering New Places!

Frame this QR with your smartphone to
Download it FOR FREE!

Introduction

Living each day of your life the way you like it is not everyone's reality. Most people work hard all their lives, make plenty of money, build houses, and acquire all sorts of expensive things, but they are not necessarily happy. What do you have to say about such people? Perhaps you are also stuck in this rut and have no clue what to do about your situation. It's not surprising or rare to find people who feel stifled in their jobs. They are probably not made for the cubicle or to work nine to five, but they do it because they have no idea how to get rid of the life they don't really enjoy. The key to happiness is simple—love what you do. No matter what you do to make a living, it should change something within you. It should make you come alive, fill you with energy, and make your heart satisfied.

If you do something that you are unhappy with, you will get frustrated, tired, and bored soon. Of course, you can take up jobs just for the money even though they do not give you real excitement or joy while you have just started out in your career. It's good to take up any kind of job just to gain experience, brush up your skills, improve your knowledge, and make money. However, you should not enslave yourself to doing something that you don't love or don't feel deeply passionate about for very long.

You can choose your own life and your destiny. The only reason for your unhappiness is your inability to decide how you want to live your life. It's all about deciding and taking action toward it. If you are clear in your mind that you want to live your life on your own terms and do exactly what makes you happy, you will find ways to create such a life.

Some people don't have the courage to quit their mundane life for a life of adventure. They spend their lives envying others and simply being miserable just because they haven't been able to muster up courage to step out and explore the unknown. On the contrary, people who are able to quit their conventional life for an unpredictable life are able to do it because they value their freedom more than anything else. Such people are not necessarily reckless or acting without a plan. In fact, they usually have a clear plan in mind and they very diligently act according to it.

Quitting your job isn't just a fantasy, like many believe it to be. It should be a responsible decision that you need to take with a lot of thought and specific planning. You should know what you are going to do and how you are going to survive without a stable job.

You need to think of ways to generate passive income for yourself. It's the only way to escape the need to work all your life. The desire to live a life of adventure without a home is not everyone's cup of tea. Most of us look for long-term planning, security, and comfort. Some people are happy doing that; however, some of us feel stuck in the conventional life that we are expected to live. So, it's time to break the traditional thought process and step out in the open sky to breathe, embrace the winds, smell the woods, feel the rain on your face, and look ahead to the open road.

This book is going to help you understand that it's okay to want to live in a motorhome instead of a house. It's okay to create your dream life. It's okay to want something more from life. You will learn ways to escape your usual, boring, and stressful life and create a life of freedom, adventure, and travel. You will also learn about various ways you can make money while traveling, meet different people, and garner beautiful memories.

You will learn about how people live a digital nomad life and embrace the laptop lifestyle. It's priceless to be location independent and be able to work from anywhere and explore various places. However, it's not devoid of challenges. So, you will also learn the ways to combat the difficulties of digital nomadism.

The ability to make money and live freely is precious, and with this book, you will learn to make it happen in a sensible way. Be warned, though! Life on the road is not so picture perfect. In fact, you will face lots of challenges; you will have to work hard. But it will give you joy, peace, satisfaction, energy, and the power to be yourself. You will also become someone who people find inspiring and would like to emulate.

Before you even begin reading this book, make sure to tell yourself that it isn't hard to create passive income. All it takes is your determination to do it, willingness to try different things, eagerness to learn, and ability to embrace the unpredictability. You will learn about different income streams that you can easily align with your motorhome lifestyle. Switching to an RV passive income lifestyle is not just about excitement and thrill, but it's also about personal growth, a lot of mental preparation, and an exceptionally rewarding life ahead.

Enjoy reading the book!

Chapter 1

How to Escape the City Stress

Quitting your job isn't something that you should recommend to anyone. However, you should do it if it's not helping you live the kind of life you truly want to live. There's no point in living in a trap. Yes, even a well-paying job can be a trap, a golden cage for many. The key point is happiness. Your life decisions should stem from what makes you happy—what inspires you, makes you feel alive, and stirs up your energy. If it's a nine-to-five job, keep doing it. But if it's not, then get out of it.

The city life is becoming more and more stressful with each passing day. Everybody seems to be running a race for no reason. Nobody is really sure of what they truly want out of their lives. Some people simply live under peer pressure or just to fulfill obligations. Sadly, some people never get to the point of discovering their own joy. They have no real goal or fervent dream in life. They wake up, brush their teeth, take a shower, put on some nice clothes, go to work, come back, have food, and go to bed. They live an insipid life, where they have no time to nurture relationships, make new friendships, pursue a hobby, explore places, or savor the beautiful things of life. But they don't seem to know the way out. Such people live a stressful life without escape because they don't allow themselves to think differently.

You don't deserve an ordinary life. You are made to live an exceptional life. But that's only possible when you choose your own originality over imitation, your purpose over obligation, and your spirit of adventure over monotony. Living a happy, meaningful, and interesting life isn't about being busy all the time, chasing targets, or making a six figure income. Sure, there's no harm in making money, but not to the point of being weighed down by it. A life of freedom and happiness is more about savoring the simpler joys of life—breathing in fresh air, enjoying the sunshine, smiling at strangers, and enjoying a good meal with your family.

Quitting a job and escaping the conventional city life may require you to change your mindset. You might have to introspect, reflect on a lot of things happening around you, and come to a point where you can make such a bold move. It's okay to feel anxious or fearful; however, you should not allow such emotions to push you back in the dungeon. You should still make the move no matter how you feel.

Before you make a move, ask yourself a few questions—"what's my true goal in life," "am I willing to learn new skills," "what makes me truly happy and alive," and "how do I see myself a decade from now." As you ask yourself these questions and answer them honestly, you will have a clear view of your life, and it will give you courage to take the plunge.

It's a good idea to analyze your present life as well. You should have no regrets later. You should not have the fear of missing out. So, give it some time and weigh the pros and cons of all possible alternatives. It's not so easy to throw a well-paying job in the trash can. You will be warned against it. It can prove to be insane if you act without a plan.

You should be aware of what you are getting into. Yes, you are about to live a dream life—a life that's going to give you meaning and purpose. You will wake up each day with excitement because you will know that you have something good to look forward to. Nobody is going to tell you what to do. You will be your own boss. There's nothing better than that, right?

Nevertheless, you will have challenges to deal with. You will have to work for every penny you earn. You will have to get rid of the "fixed income" mindset. You will need to get comfortable with the fact that you might not get your paycheck every month. You might have to wait for payments to come through. You might have to work day and night for months and do nothing at all for the rest of the year. You will live with uncertainty and yet be the happiest soul alive.

The idea of escaping the stress of city life isn't really about running away from something; it's the quest for a better life. Every human being is born to live a progressive life. We are not meant to stagnate. We are designed to become better versions of ourselves with every passing day. How do you achieve that?

Well, to get to a point where you could decide to quit your job and send everybody to hell, you need to first understand very deeply the bad effects of your stressful life. Nobody wants to live an unhappy life, right? The sad reality in today's age is that most of us don't even realize that we are unhappy. We keep doing the same stuff every day, even though it's slowly and secretly ruining us.

The main goal that we live with each day is pleasing others, doing things that are expected from us, and proving our worth to others. We don't even give ourselves one moment to pause and reflect on the things that we keep doing just because they are the accepted norms of the society. The exhausting corporate jobs, the mad city traffic, poor nutrition, sleep deprivation, media overload, and loneliness may be some of the main causes of unhappiness in your life. The problem is that most of us are unable to identify them, and we simply get into the habit of living with them.

We forget to nourish our mental health because we don't care to give it the thought and value it needs until it overpowers many of us, and then we begin to feel helpless. Let's not get to that point. Let's understand the issues that we face each day due to the mechanical life that we live. Let's not think of who to blame. Let's just identify the problems that may not look like they are very grave, but they eventually have serious consequences.

You have the right to eliminate anything that isn't giving you happiness or is simply causing you stress. If it's your job and the city life, perhaps it's time to abandon them. It has to begin with a lot of self-reflection. Don't make it a hasty decision. You need to clearly visualize the outcomes of the kind of life you are living right now and the kind of life you could live.

You also need to develop the attitude of not caring about people's opinions. Be prepared to get lots of advice against your move. You should turn a deaf ear to all the noise around you and do your own thing.

Remember, it's more difficult to keep living the monotonous life. It's far easier to escape it and find ways to sustain yourself while enjoying each day to the fullest.

So, how do you do it exactly?

You may find it overwhelming to make such a big decision all on your own. It's okay to feel jittery and even unsure in the beginning. But don't succumb to any negative feelings.

ANALYZE YOUR FINANCES

You need to take steps toward your new life. The first thing you need to do is analyze your finances. Be sure to have enough funds to sustain yourself at least for the first six months without a job. So yes, quitting your job shouldn't be an impulsive act because it could prove difficult for you and you might regret it, too. Allow yourself to come to terms with the idea of leaving a conventional lifestyle and starting something totally different.

Give it at least a few months before you actually tell your boss that you are quitting. When you have made up your mind about adapting to a nomadic lifestyle, you should start putting aside a large chunk of your income every month for at least a few months, maybe six to eight months. You might have to live on a frugal budget to save more money. It's just like planning your retirement. You will need to quit a lot of habits like buying expensive clothes, watching movies in the theater, cafe or bar hopping, and other such things. So yes, it has to be a lifestyle shift and it is going to be a slow process.

DECIDE ABOUT YOUR HOUSE AND POSSESSIONS

The next step that you should take is to consider things like your home and all your possessions. If you own a house, you need to decide if you want to sell it or rent it to someone, which can be a passive source of income for you. And, what about the stuff in your house? You should consider selling them, which is also going to add money to your bank account.

When you move to a nomadic way of life, you want to live in a minimalist fashion with only what you truly need and not with the stuff that you barely use. So, sort things out and decide what you want to keep and what you want to give away or sell.

Pay off all Your Debts

A crucial step to take before you make a move is to pay off all your pending debts, loans, or mortgages. Decide what you want to do with your credit cards. If you have been using multiple credit cards, make sure to pay them all off. You should enter into your "new" life debt-free.

Perhaps you can continue to use one or two credit cards; however, try to pay them off in full every month, so that you don't accumulate interest on any of them. As you move to a lifestyle of living in a motorhome, you want to reduce expenses, avoid paying interest on anything, make extra income, and live debt-free.

Do Your Research

You should do a lot of research and understand how exactly you will be living as a nomad. It's a totally different experience to live without a job and a permanent address. You will not have access to the usual comforts and amenities of a home. So, you want to be aware of that and plan for your life in an RV (Recreational Vehicle).

If you know of someone who has been living without a home, freelancing, and traveling in an RV, take their advice. Ask them certain practical questions, such as "how to keep getting work and maintain a cash flow," "how to deal with sickness on the road," and "how to balance work and travel." The more knowledge you have of the nomadic lifestyle, the better preparation you can have in place. So, read a lot about an RV life —the pros and cons—before you take any action.

Your Relationships and Obligations

Think about your relationships and obligations. Are you married? Do you have a family, kids, pets, or old parents to take care of? Do you live with your partner? You need to consider these things while planning for a nomadic life. You need to be sure about whether you want to make the shift alone or with somebody because that's going to change a lot of things. You can do anything alone; you can make mistakes and fall and rise up again and again. But when you are with somebody else, you need to consider the other person as well. You will need to plan and decide things together, and you will need to agree on things, or even if you disagree, it has to be done amicably.

Consider your obligations such as taking care of old parents—how are you going to ensure that they are well taken care of and that all their needs are met on time?

Test the Waters Before You Dive in

You should also research the kind of RV you want to buy. You can perhaps start with renting your house on wheels to have a taste of it before you make a purchase. You can also consider living in an RV for a couple of months while you still have your home. Instead of abandoning everything in one shot, you can make a gradual move. It's always good to test the waters before diving in.

You can also go on a trip for a month or so just to understand the kind of life an RV offers. It can be a great way to come out of your comfort zone and figure out a lot of things that you need to do every day, such as picking up groceries, cooking, laundry, and cleaning. You will get an idea of what all you really need to live comfortably in an RV. This will help you prepare for a permanent RV life.

It's good to make a move with the thought that you can always come back to your original life. You don't need to burden your mind with your decision. Yes, you want to live a life of freedom, but it comes with a cost. Therefore, you should research various income options while you still have a job.

You need to keep yourself updated to be resourceful, aware of your surroundings, and willing to learn various new things—you might have to learn a new language, new skills, or hone the skills you already have. So, as you prepare to quit your job and make a big move, you should look for ways to create income and live a sustainable RV life.

Let's look at some of the key points again—you need to sort out your finances first, downsize your expenses, become more resourceful, adapt to minimalism, decide how you want to take care of your responsibilities or obligations if you have any, and then finally get your feet wet.

You will also experience the fear of the unknown; however, the best way to deal with it is to take each day as it comes. Don't live for the future. Live for the present. Another way to reduce your anxiety is by educating yourself about the possibilities.

An RV life may not be for everyone. And, that's okay. However, if you are simply not happy with your conventional life and are tired of doing the things that have no meaning, you can break the conventions and set out. You will never find anyone telling you to live in an RV full time, so you will never really feel exactly right about it. You just have to make up your mind and stick to your decision. It has to come from within you. If you have the conviction for it, nothing can stop you and you will enjoy it.

CHAPTER 2

PREPARE YOUR MIND TO LIVE IN A MOTORHOME

NOW THAT YOU HAVE DECIDED TO LIVE IN AN RV, YOU NEED to prepare your mind for it. There will be many roadblocks, challenges, and moments of despair, but you need to be mentally strong to be able to deal with anything that may come by. It's not going to be a smooth start. It will take you some time to get used to the new life, new environment, and new work. You need to understand that traveling once in a while or even the concept of long-term travel is totally different from living in an RV and constantly moving. It's an alternative lifestyle altogether.

When you embark on your journey as a full-time RVer, you will learn a lot, and you will feel overwhelmed as you cope with a lot of new things. However, everybody starts from scratch. Nobody knows everything about an RV life without experiencing it.

You need to jump in with both your feet and embrace the discomfort to feel more confident. You need to believe in your dreams. You need to keep reminding yourself of the rewards of such a life, the excitement and thrill on the other side. Don't be surprised if you are happy and anxious at the same time. It's going to happen, and it's going to happen quite often.

It's a huge transformation that you need to undergo. It's like finding your identity all over again. You become almost a new person with a new set of ideas and priorities. The very reason that you want to escape the traditional life is that you don't want to be stuck in the hackneyed rules of the society. Thus, your choices are going to change. Each day as you wake up in your RV, you will be choosing new adventures instead of the daily grind. You will have difficulties, but they are not going to frustrate you. With each new challenge, you will learn something valuable and become a stronger individual.

The beauty of a nomadic life is hidden in its spontaneity and unpredictability. You don't know what will unfold the next moment, and that's what keeps you going. The thrill of being on the road and cruising through various landscapes is unparalleled. Sometimes you have the lushness of the forests to soothe you while sometimes you want to be hooked on the melody of the rivers. The dominance of the mountains leaves you awestruck, and you don't want to miss sleeping under the stars. Such awe-inspiring experiences are your perks and bonuses that you enjoy as you give into the serendipity of a nomadic life.

Be Aware of the Drawbacks

So, you need to have an ardent love for travel and adventure to be able to live literally on the road. You should not be choosing an RV life just because it fascinates you or one of your friends have been living like that and they seem to be the happiest of souls. You should do it only when you truly want it. You should choose it for the right reasons, and you should educate yourself about its drawbacks as well.

The more passionate and honest you are about your choice, the easier it will be for you to overcome the hardships. Yes, it's not as cushy as it looks like on social media. Everything you want to achieve will not be a piece of cake. You will not be floating on the clouds of happiness all the time. There will be moments when you will panic; you will feel clueless and helpless. You will get agitated when your WiFi connection won't work fast or there's a shortage of water while you have a pile of dirty laundry to wash.

Living in a Small Space

You should also be prepared to live in a small space because RVs are small inside. If you want to live a solo RV life, you might like it a lot. However, if you are going to share it with other people, you need to really get along with the people around you. You should be aware that it's not quite possible to get your much desired privacy while living in a motorhome with a bunch of other people. The space constraints in RVs make it hard for you to live comfortably. Therefore, you should be prepared to stock limited stuff and keep the inside space well organized.

It's Costly to Afford an RV

Another thing to be aware of is that it's quite costly to afford an RV, with the buying price ranging between $10,000 to $300,000 or more. Even financing an RV is quite expensive, and if you plan to sell your RV later, the value decreases over time.

Since RVs are not so fuel efficient, the gas costs also affect the expenses of an RV life. Not to mention the repair work for an RV can also cost a lot, which is unavoidable.

Giving up on Normal Things

Living in a motorhome also means giving up on your social life. Yes, you will meet a lot of new people along the way; however, you will not get to see your existing friends and acquaintances. Besides, you might not always have access to some of the regular things you are used to, such as television, internet connection, and mobile phone service due to lack of connectivity in some locations.

You will have to change how you meet some of the basic needs in your life, such as food, bathroom accessibility, and showers. You will not have the comfort of a hot shower whenever you like. You might have to think of ways to make certain adjustments, like taking a gym membership, which will allow you to take a shower in the gym or you can check into an Airbnb or a hotel. You will need to visualize and plan your daily routine in a motorvan.

Change Your Food Habits

You might want to change your food habits and decide what you want to have for breakfast, lunch, and dinner that you can cook on a single burner stove. You need to think of small things and be aware of what you might not have access to. For instance, it won't be a good idea to pack your blender thinking you will be making smoothies the way you do at home. However, you may consider keeping a mini fridge in your vehicle to store veggies and fruits for a week at least. Buying groceries is one of the essentials of life, which you might have to do differently from a van.

How to Prepare Your Mind for an RV Life

The idea is not to discourage you about RVing; however, you should be aware that it's not for everyone. And, if you have decided to shift gears in your life and choose to live nomadically, you should do it with a lot of mental preparedness. You can take certain simple and practical actions just to get into the groove and gain more confidence about making a big move in your life.

DECIDE on a Date to Depart

You can begin by setting a deadline for yourself for when exactly you want to set out. Of course, you cannot really decide on an exact date of departure; however, you can certainly have a rough idea about when you want to start your camper van life. It will mostly depend on the things you need to sort, such as decluttering, donating the stuff you don't need, canceling utilities, selling or renting your house, and other such things. Setting a final date of departure can infuse enthusiasm and energy in you to propel the preparation toward your goal.

Make a To-Do List

After you have decided on a tentative date, you can make a to-do list that includes researching various things like domicile residency, RVs, passive income options, insurance, and camping locations. As you keep ticking off things from your checklist, you should keep adding new things to do because you will have to think on a detailed level and come to a point where you understand the whole picture of living an RV life.

Since everybody has to deal with different situations, everybody's to-do list is also unique. So, you need to make your to-do list according to what you have in your life. Learn to simplify things by taking small daily decisions like whether to trash something or give away, to store something for later use or give it up. Have clarity in mind and take quick action. Don't keep things unattended. Schedule a daily time for decluttering and focus on small areas at a time. Don't give yourself big tasks that you know you will not be able to do in a day.

Go Paperless

You might have to change your lifestyle in a lot of ways to prepare yourself for RV life. For instance, you should make a transition to a paperless lifestyle, as it will be difficult to receive mail through the mail service. You need to get into the habit of doing all your business online or you might miss paying your bills.

Segregate Your Stuff

Be very particular about what you want to pack for your RV. You will be tempted to take everything because you might think that it's better to take along as much as you can instead of buying new stuff when needed. The truth is that you won't need most of the things that you need in your normal life. So, you need to be sure of your necessities. Nevertheless, you will make mistakes and it's okay. You need to keep telling yourself that it's okay to miscalculate and learn along the way. You don't need to be perfect. The idea is to live free, experiment, and understand what makes you happy.

You Can Start With Your Clothes

Perhaps you can start with your clothes, which will largely depend on the kind of weather you are going to be in. You need to pack clothes that are absolutely essential for the kind of location you are going to be in for at least sometime. For instance, if you are going to be in a cold place for a month or so, pack enough warm clothes. However, there has to be a basic set of clothes that you should keep with you, which could be two pairs of jeans and shorts, four to five T-shirts, a sweatshirt, and of course, your undergarments.

Kitchen Essentials

After your clothes are sorted, you can shortlist the kitchen essentials, such as a crock-pot, a couple of plates, glasses, bowls, spoons, and a bread machine if you want to bake your own bread. You may want to think about your outdoor times when you will want to sit outside the vehicle and relax with a cup of coffee and pack things like a hammock, outdoor rug, light folding chairs, and maybe a patio light.

You can take along some of your favorite things to spice up the space inside your RV—your books, some art pieces, and your family photographs.

Join RV Clubs

The more you prepare and take specific action toward the bigger picture of an RV life, the easier it will be for you to develop the right mindset.

Never shy away from seeking support from others. For instance, you can join RVing clubs to keep yourself motivated and on track about your goals. These clubs offer you great discounts on campgrounds, access to job boards, forum boards, mail service, and plenty of valuable information about an RV life, which comes straight from people who are already experiencing it, in exchange for an annual membership fee. So, it's a good idea to join such clubs and forums at least a couple of months before you leave home.

Watch or Read About Seasoned RVers

If you feel overwhelmed or clueless about a motorhome life, watch the seasoned RVers talk. Listen to what they have got to say about life on the road. It's much easier to get the real picture of a new venture when you hear about it from experts. People who have been traveling in an RV for years and years will be able to educate you about the living expenses, the fun and excitement of living in a motorhome, and how to cope with the difficulties.

Create a Vision Board

Nonetheless, there will be days when you will feel like giving up and think that all of this work preparing for life in a motorhome just isn't worth it. Perhaps you can create a vision board to combat such moments. Make a collage of different pictures that represent the kind of life you want to live—you can paste pictures of beautiful places you want to explore with a cute camper van. Looking at that vision board, you can remind yourself of the life that's waiting on the other side.

Cultivate a Community of Like-Minded People

You should also be spending more time with your family and friends as you prepare for a location independent life. Social media channels are a great way to allow your loved ones to join you on your adventure virtually. Additionally, you should also start cultivating a new community of like-minded people on Facebook or Instagram. Maybe you can start your own blog, where you can share your thoughts in an informal way and connect with people. The more you build networks, both personally and professionally, the happier you will be and the more work opportunities can come your way.

Visualize Your Life in a Motorhome

It's a great idea to think of what you anticipate in your future. Since moving to an RV full-time is a life-changing decision, it's important that you visualize your life on the road. Think about one whole day in a motorhome from morning to the time you go to sleep. Think of all the things you will do and also not do. Perhaps you will not have to worry about cooking elaborate meals or get into extensive cleaning every day. Instead, you might just step out of your campervan in the morning to watch the sunrise with a cup of coffee without thinking about the rest of the day. You may want to just settle into the day at a leisurely pace. You may want to catch up on work and then cook something quickly, take a break whenever you feel like, and relax under a tree.

The more you visualize about your RV life, the clearer your thoughts will become, and it will be much easier to make the shift.

Think About What You Hate About Your Current Life

No matter how much you hate your current life, it's not easy to make a transition into something new. There's a comfort zone that you are used to. Many people keep grumbling about various things that they are unhappy about, but very few choose to do something to change their circumstances. If you are frustrated about your work life, the stress of the city, and the way you feel every day, you should think of ways to improve your life. You may think of changing your job or moving to a different neighborhood, but that's not going to help in the long run. You need to get down to the root of the problem, which is that you are seeking something much more meaningful than what your traditional life could ever give. Thus, you have chosen the path of being a digital nomad, creating passive income, living in a campervan, and enjoying freedom every single day of your life.

It's Okay to be Different

You might have people in your life who are going to tell you that what you have decided is insane and that you will get bored very soon and return to your original life. You need to tell yourself that it's okay even if you do fail at it. You need to constantly remind yourself that it's okay to be different and want to live in a certain way. The key is to be happy even when nothing out of the ordinary is happening.

The problem in our conventional life is that everybody is just waiting for something big to happen or a circumstance to change. But that never happens really. That's why most people live frustrated lives. You are the courageous one to change the course of your life and dare to do something different.

Go on Trial Runs

Lastly, go on trial runs before you finally bid adieu to your home, office, and your usual life. Plan a camper sojourn for a month or so and see if you like it enough to live that way for an extended period of time. Trial runs will give you the real picture of an RV life and will help you know what to take along and what to discard without a second thought.

Another thing to do is to live in your motorhome full-time but not away from your hometown for at least a month. It's good to make a slow transition to be able to deal with the challenges of an RV life easily.

Stay aligned to your own conviction and you will always be on the right path and have the right mindset.

CHAPTER 3

HOW TO MANAGE YOUR MONEY SO THAT IT GROWS

LET'S FACE IT, MONEY IS THE BACKBONE OF EVERYTHING WE do in life. You can't live the life of your dreams without money. Everybody needs money no matter what they want to make of their lives. Whether you desire to live in a big house all your life or set out on an unplanned adventure, money is at the center of it all. However, it's not really about being rich or poor. It's all about managing your money well and having a mindset to make more money. Some people are satisfied with whatever money they make; they neither intend to save money nor create more of it. They just live the way they have been living without much ambition, which is fine for those who want to live that way.

However, to live a life of freedom, beauty, and adventure, you need lots of money. The sooner you accept it, the easier it's going to be for you to find ways to make money. The only way to get rid of the need to work all your life is to manage your money well while you are still young and obtain financial stability at an age when you just want to savor each moment without worrying about your next meal.

Some people live with the notion that wanting to make more money is being greedy. But that's far from the truth. You need to remind yourself that everything in life comes with a cost. There are no free lunches in the world; so, wanting to make extra money is a wise way of thinking. Now, all you need is the right approach to it. Most people lose money or are unable to grow their wealth because they have no clue how to manage their money. They are not aware of the right saving or investing options and strategies; they don't care to learn them, either. Some people make lots of money, but they blow it all on useless things and at the wrong places, which means they completely mismanage their money.

If you have the desire to grow rich and live freely, you need to learn how to manage your money and make even more money. There's no harm in having multiple sources of income. Remember, a life of adventure and travel demands a lot of money. However, the beautiful part is that you never grow poor when you travel and experience new things. Travel makes you richer with experiences, memories, and wisdom.

Be Aware of Your Expenses

So, keep your eyes wide open and nurture dreams in them! The first step to managing your earning well is being aware of your expenses. You should spend your money mindfully. If you are shopping, you should do it with awareness. If you are having a pizza in an expensive restaurant, you should be mindful of it. Being aware doesn't mean just knowing what you are doing. Being aware or being mindful means to think about your thoughts, desires, will, intention, and actions on a deeper level and be conscious of the outcome.

When you are aware that buying an expensive watch is not going to serve any real purpose in life, and it's just a style statement that's not going to give you any joy in the long run, you keep yourself from buying it. That's how you get into the habit of spending right. That being said, you don't always have to deprive yourself of luxuries and live only on essentials. You should pamper and treat yourself once in a while, when you are convinced about your desires. However, spending mindlessly most of the time is never going to take you anywhere.

Save and Invest

The second step to managing your money right is to save and invest. Have an organized approach to saving and investing. In fact, the best way to keep a tight hold on your purse strings is to put aside at least 40% of your income for savings and keep the rest for expenses. Of course, it's not possible for many of us to save a huge amount of their income every month, as there are so many necessary expenses to meet. So, you can save whatever amount you are comfortable with.

Most of us start with expenses and are left with almost nothing at the end of a month. You should do the opposite and start with allocating a large part of your income toward savings and some sort of investment first before you budget out your expenses. If you fall in the age group of 18 to 30, you should be investing more and saving less, and if you come under the age group of 31 to 45 (and above), you should save more and invest modestly. When you are young, you can afford to be a little aggressive with your investments because you have time to recover your losses and you have comparatively fewer liabilities to take care of.

Don't Pay Interest on Your Money

The third approach to money management is to safeguard your money, which means not keeping too many credit cards or loans. Don't pay interest on money. It's the biggest trap that most of us easily fall into. Keep your life free of credit cards, if possible. If not, use them sparingly and always pay them in full. Believe it or not, saying no to credit cards is the smartest way to live. You will save yourself from a lot of trouble and live much more peacefully. Don't think of spending yet. First, earn your money, then save and invest some, and then go out and spend.

Keep an Emergency Fund

Don't keep all your money blocked in savings and investments. Keep a certain portion of it as liquid cash, which you can use whenever you are in need. You should keep your emergency fund separate and it should be easily withdrawable. Now, the question is: how much should you put aside for an emergency? Ideally, it should be your salary of at least six months if not more. Building an emergency fund is a good practice, which you should start early in your life, perhaps as soon as you start working.

Make Financial Goals

The way you manage your finances should also reflect your short- and long-term goals in life. Make financial goals and write them down, so that they are imprinted on your mind and you can work on fulfilling them. Don't be random about your finances. Be specific about how much you want to save and what kind of life you want to live after five years or a decade from now.

You should also have short-term savings for traveling or buying electronics. You may save for a year or so and then splurge on your favorite destination or the latest iPhone. The reason why you may buy an expensive smartphone is because it's going to support you in living as a digital nomad. With a good smartphone, you can stay active on social media, take beautiful pictures, make videos, and do a lot more interesting stuff. So, a good phone is a wise investment. So yes, save for the things you want to buy or the experiences you want to garner.

Your long-term savings could be for financial stability after retirement; it could be to sustain yourself when you want to quit your regular job or do a world tour. Whatever may be the case with you, the idea is to save as much as possible. Also, save for a rainy day. Don't keep all your money blocked, though. Keep an emergency fund, which should be liquid, and it should be able to take care of you for at least six months.

As far as investments are concerned, many people feel perplexed about them, and they keep themselves from becoming rich. You don't have to acquire any skills to be a good investor. All you need is patience and a little knowledge of what's going on in the market. Remember, you get rich slowly. Most people have the wrong notions about becoming rich by investments—they believe it's some stroke of luck that can make them rich overnight. But that doesn't happen. You need to invest and wait to see your money grow and not gamble and lose your money. Yes, investments of any kind have risks involved. No financial investment is devoid of risk. However, when you invest in small amounts periodically, it evens out the highs and lows of the market.

Create Financial Assets

To be able to afford a long-term nomadic life, you should focus on creating financial assets, such as real estate, land, precious metals, bonds, or stocks while you are still making a fixed income. Such financial assets can serve as passive income for you. Besides, you can always sell them when their value increases and make more money. Yes, you do need to evaluate their value before you sell any of your assets. Never be in a hurry to sell off anything that has an appreciating value. Wait for the right time to get the real value of what you have in store.

However, you need a disciplined approach to create long-term wealth for yourself. Perhaps you will need to have the mindset of an investor from day one, as soon as you start earning. You might have to downsize your expenses and adapt to a modest lifestyle even when everyone around you is partying every weekend or buying expensive cars.

Budget Out Your Expenses

You might find it hard to have a spending budget in place, but it can help you keep track of your money. Make a list of the absolute expenses that you cannot do without and try to understand how much money you need to meet those expenses; then make a list of expenses that are not necessary but give you pleasure, such as movies, coffee, or clubbing and try to figure out how much money you need for them. There's no harm in indulging in expensive things occasionally as long as you do them with awareness and not out of sheer impulsiveness. It's always good to write things down somewhere to have more clarity and make better decisions.

Never Increase Expenses When Your Pay Increases

The wisest thing to do with your personal finances is to never increase expenses when your income increases. When you get a raise in your salary, keep your expenses as they were before you started receiving a higher paycheck. Most of us have the natural tendency to start spending more money just because there's more cash flow. However, it's the silliest thing to do. The better decision is to keep the excess aside and allow it to grow. For instance, if your income has grown by 25% in a year, keep it aside and don't even consider it as part of your income. The thing with savings and investments is that the growth is slow as you start; however, it's quite rapid in the later years. The exponential growth happens only after you have invested a lot of your patience through the years.

When you buy things on interest, you pay extra money, and it turns out to be much more than the actual price of the commodity. On the contrary, when you save or invest money, you earn interest, which also turns out to be huge due to its compounding power. So, be aware of how you operate with your money. Have your pick!

Look out for Additional Income

Additionally, you should always be looking out for additional ways of making money. The more money you make, the better life you can afford later and you can enjoy the luxury of not working. These days, it's not so difficult to find different revenue streams as long as you have the skills to research and reach out to people. Don't live in your own cocoon and expect people to find you. Be out there to be seen and approached for work. You need to package yourself in a way that the right opportunities knock on your doors.

You may want to do some petty jobs like washing cars or running errands to make some extra income or you may want to utilize your special skills such as writing, photography, painting, teaching, or coaching. Whatever it is, just do it!

Get serious about your personal finances. Have a plan in place and act every day toward it. Live modestly, save, invest, create assets, allow your money to grow, and create extra income. The secret to being rich is being disciplined about your money.

CHAPTER 4

BUSINESSES FOR AN RV LIFE

WHEN YOU SET OUT TO LIVE IN A VEHICLE AND HAVE FEWER worries, you should be open to all kinds of money-making prospects. Of course, this means prospects that are fair and legal. You should also be open to experimenting with your capabilities. You may even surprise yourself by doing certain jobs that you never thought you would be able to do. For instance, if you are impatient with kids and you end up babysitting, it would make you smile and feel proud of yourself. Wouldn't that be fun? The idea is to challenge yourself, try different things, meet all sorts of wonderful people, and grow.

There are certain kinds of businesses that are ideal for an RV life, which you should think about and explore to find which would be the best for you. You may enjoy some of them while detest the others. It's up to you what you choose. However, whatever you do, make sure it aligns with your motorhome lifestyle and that you have enough time to explore the world, because that's what you really want to do. Each job that you take up should give you an experience, teach you something of value, and make you a better individual.

You can pick more than one job from the many options available or you can simply do one and be happy.

Babysitting

Let's start with babysitting, a job that anyone can do. All you need is the ability to care for kids. You don't have to be of a certain age or have a certain qualification to do it. Yes, you do need to be trained to babysit, which is essential. You should know basic safety and first aid and how to tackle common emergencies. You need to understand that parents are going to trust you with their children, so you will need to assure them you know your job well.

To start with, get trained in first aid and CPR (cardiopulmonary resuscitation), which will help you beat the competition and charge more. You should also learn about child behavior and how to discipline them.

It's not so hard to find babysitting jobs, as there are many channels of exposure, such as networking, referrals, job sites, and of course, everyone's favorite—you can put the word out on social media that you are available as a babysitter. Don't forget to tell your friends and family about your babysitting skills, as even they might be looking out for your services. You can be seen at playgrounds and kids' birthday parties to introduce yourself! Not to mention you should sign up on websites like Care.com and SitterCity.

You will find that job postings have specific requirements, such as the hourly wage and rules with respect to your phone usage, meal preparation, driving requirements, and assistance with homework.

The best way to find babysitting jobs is to sign up with popular apps like UrbanSitter, eNannySource, SitterCity, Bambino, and others. Additionally, you can check out bulletin boards in community centers, gyms, and coffee shops. You may also want to engage in moms' groups on Facebook and check out moms' clubs and church groups. You never know where you might find your client.

You can easily make somewhere between $10 to $20 per hour as a babysitter. Your pay depends on your experience and qualifications, so make sure to get yourself a certificate if you plan to pursue babysitting professionally.

Foreign Language Coaching

Another great job for a motorhome life is foreign language coaching or online teaching. All you need is command over a language—most companies look for native speakers and prior experience in teaching a language. If you fit the bill, you can teach English online to anybody across the globe.

But can you teach English without a degree? Yes, you can! Although there are some big online teaching organizations that ask for a degree to teach English, there are many who let you in without a certification. Since the job market is pretty competitive, it's good to enroll in a TEFL (Teaching English as a Foreign Language) course to secure online English teaching jobs easily. The companies that do not require you to have a degree to teach English online are PalFish, Lingoda, Open English, Cambly, Verbling, and SkimaTalk, just to name a few.

The easiest way to begin teaching English online is via an app—you can choose one of the language learning online apps like HelloTalk, HiNative, or Meetup. Yes, you will need to have good internet connectivity because you will be teaching via video calls. You should also have a headset with a microphone and preferably a good webcam. And of course, you cannot teach in a noisy or an underlit environment. Thus, you need to ensure you have a quiet space with the appropriate background and lighting for teaching. You should be aware that there are companies that will ensure you have proper lighting.

So, how much can you make in a month by just teaching a language online? Well, you can decide how much you want to charge. If you are qualified and experienced, you should start at a high rate because people value something more when it's hard to afford and take it for granted when it's cheap or free. So, you can make anything between $30 to $50 per hour by teaching a language online. However, these rates are not fixed. You should do your own research and speak to experts before you set your own teaching price.

SELLING YOUR OWN ONLINE COURSES

Now, let's move onto another way of making money while traveling—which is to create online courses. If you are an expert in a particular subject, you can create your own courses, convert them into a series of videos, and upload them on platforms like Udemy, Domestika, and Teachable.

You need to begin by thinking of a topic that you know deeply about; it could be anything that people care about—blogging, writing, social media, digital marketing, SEO, personal finances, photography, music, art, cooking, fitness, self-development, and so on. The list is endless. You need to understand what you know all about, or at least a great deal about, that you want to share with the world.

The key to choosing the right topic for creating a course is to see if it's in demand. Your course should be able to add value to certain people's lives and help them reach their goals and eventually make money just like you do. After you have decided on a topic, create its outline and start writing the course. Do the required research and come up with the best content possible. Don't aim at making your course too lengthy or complicated, as it's not going to work. You need to understand why people prefer to learn online—because they want to learn at their own pace and within the comforts of their home. Everybody likes to learn things in the easiest way possible. So, you need to focus on giving value and not length.

As soon as your course material is ready, you will need to make videos where you will be talking to your students and teaching them what you have prepared. To do that, you will need a conducive video-making environment; you can shoot videos with your phone camera or use a webcam, a microphone, and maybe a tripod. As mentioned earlier, you can upload your complete course on one of the platforms of your choice.

Now comes the most crucial aspect of creating a course, which is the pricing—how should you price your online course? The usual thought process that most of us go through is that the lower the price, the easier it is to make a sale. But that's not true. You need to price your course based on factors like how practical and comprehensive it is, how much it's going to help your students in achieving their goals, and of course, you also need to understand your own value and authority in the market. The bottomline is that you should never price your courses too low!

It's a simple strategy to understand, which says that if you price something too low, it automatically loses its value. For instance, people usually pick up a low-priced book and barely read it. Besides, it's always easier to generate more revenue with a high price point—when you have priced your course at $100 and you make 10 sales, your total earnings are going to be $1000, while if you price your course at $500 and you make five sales, you will make $2,500. That being said, you need to price your courses sensibly and use fair judgment.

Being a Virtual Assistant to Somebody

Another job that's of high value these days is a virtual assistant. As the name suggests, the job requires you to help somebody virtually—you can be anywhere in the world and take care of administrative jobs on behalf of somebody else. For instance, if you need to assist a digital entrepreneur, you will probably be sending out emails, researching, creating marketing campaigns, making phone calls, managing social media, and maintaining calendars for them.

The good news is that there isn't any special expertise or qualification you need to be someone's virtual assistant. All you need is some experience in the particular field you want to assist somebody in and loads of enthusiasm. Needless to say, you need to be highly organized, disciplined, and internet-savvy as well as have great communication and interpersonal skills. And virtual assistants make a lot of money! Yes, you can charge an hourly rate or a flat rate. However, it's better to charge according to the number of hours you are going to invest in a week. For instance, you can start by charging anywhere between $20 to $50 per hour depending on the kind of services you provide your client.

Customer Service

Now, let's talk about being a customer service representative. You can also make money by solving people's queries while living in a motorhome. To be a customer service representative, you need to be a great listener, a peacemaker, a creative thinker, and someone who's able to meet a customer's needs. Although customer service representatives typically work in call centers, their workplace can be anywhere with the latest communication technology. It works as a location independent career because the job simply requires you to communicate digitally and not see somebody in person—neither the customer nor your team members. So, as a customer care representative, you can function via a digital communication medium and abjure going to a traditional office, which is awesome.

Take Freelance Assignments

You can take up freelance work in various fields, such as writing, editing, translation, graphic design, web design, video editing, and others. To find freelance projects, you can sign up on platforms like Fiverr, Upwork, Freelancer, and Behance, to name a few. They usually pay you an hourly rate or a fixed rate depending on the project and the scope of work. You may take work as your schedule allows and make money while traveling. However, you should not limit your approach to just the mentioned platforms. The more experience you gain, the better clients you can get access to provided you research well and network at the right places, such as LinkedIn and Facebook groups.

Freelancing proves to be more prolific when you have a good portfolio of work available digitally for your potential clients to see. That is why it's good to start your own blog and create a strong social media presence. Most people make money because of their blog and not necessarily via their blog. Yes, of course, you can monetize your blog after a point—you can place affiliate marketing links, run ads, write branded content, and sell your own products. However, what's even more appealing is that your blog serves as your digital portfolio, which helps you grab more work.

START YOUR OWN BLOG

So, what should you blog about? It doesn't matter what you choose to blog about; however, what you should ensure is that you are consistent and deliver a certain kind of content every time. You need to stick to a niche topic rather than write about different niches. The reason you should not wander away from your niche is because your audience begins to follow your blog for a particular topic, which could be anything—travel, food, technology, fashion, or fitness. For instance, you can write a blog about an RV life and ways to create passive income. Your readers will be able to relate to your blogs because you will be sharing from your own experiences. Your blog should be about something that you are passionate about, have personally experienced, and have succeeded at.

BECOME A SOCIAL MEDIA INFLUENCER

You can be a social media influencer to generate some income for you. While it's not so easy to create a stable income from social media, it can be a great way to connect with different brands and build a community of like-minded people. Social media has evolved over the years, and now it's a huge channel to network and show your work on. So, whether you make money via social media or not, you can still use it to promote your blog and your skills as well as connect with a variety of people.

If you are someone who enjoys making videos, you should devote some time to Instagram and post reels and IGTV videos. You can collaborate with various brands and make money. The more followers you have, the easier it gets to be seen by big brands who pay well.

Manage Social Media Accounts for Others

Many successful social media influencers also make money by managing social media accounts for different brands. It's a virtual job, which can be done from anywhere. Thus, any brand who wants to grow their following on various social media channels is likely to hire you as their social media manager. However, you need to be clear about your deliverables and communicate to the brand what you will be able to accomplish and what you will not do. For instance, there are brands who might just want somebody to keep their social media accounts active and connect with relevant people; they might not be looking for a mass following, whereas there are brands that specifically ask for growth in the number of followers. So, you need to charge according to your deliverables, the strategies you will be implying, and the time you are going to devote.

Offer Travel Consultancy Services

There are people who don't enjoy travel planning at all. They hate to research or find ways to travel cheap. They don't want to take on the headache of shortlisting a destination, looking for discounted deals, picking the best sightseeing options or eating places, creating an itinerary, and figuring out when and how to go. That's where you are needed as a travel consultant to help such people plan their travel. You can make their travel memorable by applying your expertise and knowledge.

You may charge on an hourly basis or you may charge a flat fee depending on your client's requirements and the time you are going to devote to the job.

Consider Investing in NFTs, Cryptos, and Stocks

You should also consider betting on NFTs, cryptocurrencies, and stocks to create some extra wealth. You may find these terms a bit intimidating in the beginning; however, as you begin to study them and experiment with at least one of these, you will find them worth your time and efforts.

Let's understand what an NFT is—it's a non-fungible token that records the ownership of a unique digital content—it could be in the form of videos, images, songs, paintings, drawings, or essays. So, a unique digital content can be used or downloaded by many, but it can be owned by only one person. The digital artwork comes with a digital ownership, which can be bought or sold. For instance, if you are a budding artist, you too can convert your own digital art to an NFT and sell it. So, it's just like betting on an asset and waiting to see if its market value increases with time or not. If the digital art piece that you have the ownership of grows in demand, you can sell the ownership to somebody else at a higher price and secure a lot of extra money.

Now, what is cryptocurrency and why is everyone going crazy about it? Well, if you study it deeply and understand how it works, you can make a steady income by investing in cryptos. It's a kind of digital asset, which is encrypted and decentralized, which means it's not managed by any central authority. The value of cryptocurrency is determined by its users who are spread across many computers around the world. Although crypto can be used to purchase regular goods and services, it's usually used as an investment asset just like stocks or precious metals.

The first thing you need to keep in mind while buying a cryptocurrency is that its value is highly volatile, and if you put in a huge amount of money in it without any knowledge or understanding, you might lose your money. So, make a slow start—invest a small amount of money just to get a hang of it, and as you gain confidence, you can start putting in more money.

WORKING AS AN RV TECHNICIAN

If you are able to adjust to a motorhome lifestyle and you think it's going to be a passion with you for a long, long time, you can take up quite a few RV jobs, such as working as an RV technician. You will get to know a lot of folks who are RVing just like you, and as they face some technical issues with their vans, they might need a repair service. You can announce to them that you are available.

RENT OR SELL YOUR RV

You can also rent or sell your RV and make money. Perhaps after spending a year or two in an RV, you can upgrade to a better one and sell the one you have. Some people also flip RVs as a business, which means they refurbish the old, dilapidated RV and make it look completely new. However, you need to check and see a few things before you put your RV on sale—the condition of engine, oil level, tires, water damage, frame damage, gas tanks, and all the interiors. You can then place it on sale on platforms like Facebook Marketplace or RVTrader.com. When it comes to pricing your much-driven RV, you should determine it by understanding the requirements of your potential buyers and then matching it up with the kind of space your vehicle has. For instance, if your motorhome has four to six beds, you can sell it to a big family and if it has two beds, you can target a couple. So, your pricing will largely depend on the kind of people who are going to buy your RV. If you aim it at a young couple, you might have to bring down the price because they might not have a big budget. However, if you try to sell it to a retiree, who wants to make an RV their permanent home and travel full-time, you might strike a good deal with them, as they are likely to invest in a good RV.

As far as renting an RV is concerned, it can be a great surplus income for you. You can make anything between $30,000 to $60,000 per year by renting your RV. However, it largely depends on the kind of RV you have—whether it's a simple and basic one or a luxurious one.

It's easier to rent a Class A motorhome, which is quite spacious on the inside and can accommodate multiple people, than a basic motorhome like a campervan. While Class A motorhomes are more expensive, they are able to retain their value better. Thus, clients who rent such luxurious RVs take care of them well, too.

You should also be aware that renting an RV isn't really a passive income, because you need to constantly work at maintaining it. From power washing the outside to wiping down the inside, there's plenty of cleaning to be done post each trip.

Sell Products at Flea Markets, Festivals, and RV Shows

There's no limit to how you can make some extra bucks while experiencing an RV life. You can sell various kinds of goods and merchandise at RV shows, festivals, fairs, and flea markets. If you are a professional artist, maybe it's a good opportunity for you to exhibit your art in front of many audiences. You can make your own handmade products, paintings, sketches, and potteries, and showcase them at exhibitions and fairs.

You can sell anything from jewelry to car wash products at such trade shows and rallies. But what's more important is that you have a niche and an audience for it. So, you need to be focused about it and plan ahead.

Take up a Seasonal Job at Amazon CamperForce

What else can you do to get some extra cash flowing? You can work as an Amazon CamperForce, which is a unique way of making money seasonally while RVing full-time. You need to work in a warehouse and do jobs like packing, sorting, picking, receiving, handling packages, and ICQA (Inventory Control & Quality Assurance). If you are roped in through the CamperForce program, you are required to live in your RV, in an RV park or campground, for as long as your contract is active.

You have a choice to work full-time as well as part-time. You get paid at an hourly rate, which is a minimum of $15 per hour, and that is paid to you at the end of each week. Then, you also receive a weekly allowance known as "CampPay" to pay for your campsite fees. You have a chance to make some extra bucks by working overtime and not to mention you are eligible for an end-of-season bonus, too.

Workamping

It's no surprise that there's a growing trend of people adapting to the full-time work camper lifestyle, which helps them fulfill their dream of traveling to various places. Anybody can be a work camper—you can be a retiree, single, or a couple. Most of the work camper jobs require you to have your own motorhome.

Workamping simply means to work and camp at the same time. It's a fantastic combination for RVers for many reasons—they get a free campsite and they get paid for the job they do while RVing. There are all sorts of jobs available for you as a camper—you can work as a receptionist, campground host, technician, craft show vendor, park ranger, tour guide, photographer, security guard, and so on.

As a workamper, you can typically make up to $7.25 to $9.00 per hour. Depending on the kind of position you work for, you can even make somewhere between $12 to $20 per hour. Of course, the higher you get paid, the more work hours you need to put in and the more responsibility. So, you can choose the kind of work that suits your schedule and priorities.

Converting Half of Your Vehicle Into a Food Truck

You can also create a business on the go and generate an income for yourself by converting half of your vehicle into a food truck. The concept of half food truck and half RV works for many camp dwellers.

So, how do you do it? You can convert half of your vehicle into a food truck by measuring the available size, deciding the layout, cutting the cardboard sheets, making drawers and shelves, attaching steel brackets, adding a refrigerator, ovens, garbage disposal equipment, and connecting the electrical supply. You need to make sure you have all the facilities required for cooking, selling the food, and perhaps a small seating area for your customers. It's definitely a fun way of making money because you feed people with delicious food and also interact with them. There's lots of energy and buzz around the van. And, if food is a passion with you, it won't even feel like work. However, it's a business that involves some expenses as you establish it and as you run it. Additionally, a food business of any kind is highly demanding and requires a lot of your time and effort. So, you need to be prepared for that before you get your hands dirty.

You need to prepare a checklist of things that you need to do for your RV food truck business, such as studying a food concession manual and understanding all health, safety, and food handling codes, equipment specifics, and rules for running a mobile food truck business. You should also check the interiors of your RV carefully and see if you need to deconstruct any area, make changes, add anything, or remove anything. You will need to redesign and make your motorhome apt for your food business.

Be aware that you will be spending money on legal formalities, such as licenses and permits, and then there are inventory and operational costs, which are ongoing costs. However, converting your partial RV into a food truck is comparatively cheaper than opening a traditional restaurant.

After you have made all the necessary changes to your RV, you need to complete the required licensing process and allow the health department to inspect the concession vehicle. They are going to let you know if there are any issues with your RV that you must address before you kick-start your food business.

Now, when you sit down to decide your menu, you should consider a few simple points, such as that the food should be easy to eat; no silverware or tables should be needed.

Your kitchen is going to be small, which means you will need to work in a super organized way to be able to cook fast if there are lots of orders pouring in. In some cases, like if you want to run a bakery truck, you can prepare your dishes ahead of time to reduce your cooking when you have to make something on the spot. Nevertheless, it's always better to be able to cook on-demand for more popularity and sales.

The best part about running a motorhome food truck business is that you can move to attract more visitors and you can experiment with your location. If your business doesn't do well at a particular place, you can move to some other place and see if it works. So yes, there is flexibility, scope for lots of creativity, and lots of fun in having your own food truck!

That being said, you need to be aware that the food business is not for everyone. You need to have certain skills in cooking, business, market understanding, and customer service to be able to succeed at such a fast-paced business.

No matter what you do to make a living in your RV, just be aware of the unstable nature of all such jobs. When you are living in a motorhome, nothing is permanent, but that's what appeals to you, right? So, keep reminding yourself of your real purpose in life and keep looking out for work and make additional income streams to sustain yourself long-term.

Below are a couple of books that you can read to learn more about making an income while RVing:

- NFT for Beginners by Brendon Fowler

The Most Updated Non Fungible Tokens Guide. Discover How to Fill Your Pockets With Cryptocurrency & Blockchain. Start Investing in Digital Art & Create Your own Collectibles Now!

- Food Truck Business Guide by Romeo Farrel

Plan a Dynamic Strategy and Achieve Success Selling Food on Four Wheels. Bring Your Dream Job to Life Making Customers Happy. Conquer Smorgasburg With Your Cooking Skills!

Chapter 5

How to Become a Digital Nomad

Becoming a digital nomad is one of the most exciting ways to live, particularly if you combine it with an RV life. Wouldn't you agree? A digital nomad is someone who works through technology and is location independent. All you need to become a digital nomad is fast internet connection and a laptop. Yes, it's that simple. However, strong internet availability is not always feasible, especially if you are traveling in remote places. So, you need to plan your work in a way that it gets done on time even when there isn't much connectivity.

So, who's a digital nomad? You are a digital nomad if you are a freelance writer, designer, coder, YouTuber, blogger, or a digital entrepreneur. You don't need to show up physically and do your work sitting in a cubicle looking at your boss' office. It's completely the opposite of what a normal work environment looks like—as a digital nomad, you can work from your motorhome peeping out to a beautiful view, sipping coffee, and listening to your favorite playlist. You can get up and do some stretches as your mind wanders and you find it hard to focus. If you aren't feeling productive in a certain moment, maybe you can shut down your laptop and go for a walk by the beach, come back with renewed energy and an upbeat mood, and start working again. So, there's plenty of flexibility in a digital nomad's life. Nevertheless, flexibility doesn't mean lack of discipline. If you need to devote a certain number of hours and get a job done within a timeframe, you have to do it. It's just that you can choose your work hours and days. You may work on a Sunday while take an off on a Monday. It's totally up to you.

A digital nomad life or a laptop lifestyle is truly fascinating. It has many benefits for sure. Apart from the freedom and flexibility you get, there's also no limit to how much money you can make. Is there anything better than rolling in cash while watching the crashing sea waves from your RV window? The beauty and uniqueness of digital nomadism is staying connected to your favorite things while earning an income. On the contrary, when you are stuck in an office building, you work in a confined space, which limits your thoughts and vision as well. You work under pressure or under fear, but when you allow yourself to work from anywhere, it opens up your mind and makes you think more actively and deliver better work. The idea of being your own boss is what makes it so appealing and truly satisfying.

You can work from a beach, where the romance of salty winds will keep you inspired; you can work while swaying in a hammock listening to the chirps of birds, in the midst of a forest taking in the verdure, or in a remote countryside smelling the fragrant produce. It's a beautiful experience to be able to work from any location of your choice. Therefore, the thrill of working never fades away. In fact, it's a growing trend. Everybody wants to be location independent when it comes to work.

Everybody desires flexibility in terms of work schedules, and everybody wants to incorporate a dash of creativity in their daily work routine. Even though the traditional way of working still exists and it may exist forever, as there are certain jobs that require your physical presence, the idea of remote working or laptop lifestyle is being enthusiastically accepted across the globe.

As someone who wants to live in a motorhome full-time and make an income, digital nomadism is the solution for you. Yes, of course, you can take up seasonal work and many camper jobs that require you to be in the field, but you should definitely aim at being a full-time digital nomad as well. Camper life and digital nomadism are a good match. The only hitch is the weak internet connectivity in some areas, which may hamper your work. However, there are ways to combat that and still manage to do your work without any delays.

You will get into situations where you will not have access to the internet. You may experience slow internet connectivity, which is frustrating but tolerable. Sometimes, it will take you longer than usual to finish an assignment. There are various factors responsible for bad internet connection—it could be the weather, such as thunderstorms or rains; it could be a remote location where the signals are usually weak or your internet service provider may not be serving yet. Whatever be the cause, you need to be aware of the internet issues and be resourceful about resolving them and working things out for yourself.

How to Get Access to Good Internet Connectivity

So, how to ensure that you are able to work as a digital nomad in a motorhome or while traveling? There are quite a few tips and tricks to follow to avoid disruptions and maintain the workflow.

Look for Internet Options Ahead in Time

Don't arrive in a new place and wonder what to do about internet connectivity. That's bad work planning. If you don't want any work disruptions, you should ensure that the place you are visiting has good

WiFi connectivity. If you are planning to work from your campervan, you may consider buying local sim cards in the town or city you are in and you can use your phone's hotspot to get internet connectivity.

You will easily get WiFi at places like airports, hotels, Airbnbs, restaurants, and cafes; however, how strong the internet connectivity is going to be is not definite. If you plan to stay in a hotel or an Airbnb for a few days, you can call up your host and inquire about the WiFi speed they offer. If it's not fast enough, you should consider upgrading your internet plan on your phone.

Don't Visit Remote Places When You Have a Deadline to Meet

It doesn't make sense to travel to places with no connectivity while you are loaded with work. Finish your work while you are still in a good network so that you can travel with no work stress. It's not always practical to mix work and travel. It's better to enjoy traveling and forget about work than to struggle with slow internet.

You need to strike a balance between your work and travel, which is possible only when you decide when you are able to not work for a few days. Since work is a priority, you need to plan your travel around it and not vice versa.

Park Your RV Close to the WiFi Source

If you are in a campground and trying to access the WiFi of the campground office, try to be in close proximity to the connection source to get the best signal quality and speed. Being at a distance from the WiFi source is never a good idea. You can also try going out of the vehicle to check if the signal improves.

So, maybe you need a bit of planning and strategy to ensure you are always close to WiFi signals.

Get an External Wireless Card

You can ensure good internet connectivity with an external wireless card, at least to some extent. Since it has a strong transmitter and antenna, you will find access to more available networks other than your laptop, which will lead to faster connection. You can plug the card into your laptop via USB.

Remove Unnecessary Apps on Your Mobile

If you are using data from your mobile plan to get the internet, you should check if there are apps that are using your data and hampering connectivity. Sometimes your smartphone apps run in the background and consume a lot of your data when you aren't even using them. It's always good to remove media files that you don't want, apps that are not required, and even spam emails. Keep your phone and laptop memory clean, so that your devices work smoothly and your internet connectivity is better.

Use Speedify for Multiple Connections

Now, you can have the best available network with Speedify. Its channel bonding technology combines multiple networks and allows you to have access to the fastest internet. So, if one connection weakens, you automatically get access to the stronger one. Quite awesome, right? It can be any kind of connection—wired, wi-fi, cellular, or an ethernet connection. The technology combines the bandwidth to give you a faster internet speed immediately.

Buy a Pair of Noise-Canceling Headphones

As a digital nomad, you might have to work in different places, sometimes even in unconventional environments, such as a busy restaurant or next to a train station. It's easy to lose focus in a public place, where everybody is muttering something. Thus, you should use noise-canceling headphones and put the buzz around you on mute.

Use a VPN

Getting a good WiFi connection shouldn't be your only concern as a digital nomad; you should also be worried about your personal information that you share on various public WiFi networks. Your personal messages, emails, banking details, and other data can be accessed and misused by anybody. Thus, you need to protect your information by getting a reputed virtual private network (VPN), which ensures that your online data is safe.

DON'T GET INTO THE TRAP OF OVERWORKING

While digital nomadism is awesome and has many benefits, it can start ruling your life. If you are not mindful about it, you will end up checking your phone every now and then. You may feel tempted to check your Instagram the moment you wake up or your email just before you go to bed, which is extremely unhealthy for your overall life. You need to set boundaries for yourself right from the start. You should define your work hours, screen time, and rest and recreation time to enjoy life in balance.

If you allow work to take away all your time, energy, and emotions, then you will be unknowingly going back to your old corporate grind lifestyle. The idea of quitting your regular job and switching to an RV life is to create work-life balance and to enjoy being who you are. You don't have to be a workaholic to accomplish yourself as a successful digital nomad. So, take it easy and savor every bit of your life on the road.

Being a Digital Nomad While Living in an RV

You can add to the joy of being a digital nomad and make the whole experience more meaningful by integrating certain ideas and strategies. You need to be aware that there are many challenges of a digital nomad life. It's not as dreamlike as it may look like in Instagram posts. Digital nomads from all across the globe make it look like a dream job—you are working from a treehouse sipping away beer. Well, that's true. However, that's just one side of the whole picture. In reality, a digital nomad has to deal with slow internet, work long hours, and even stay back in their hotel room to attend a business meeting while their friends might be chilling at the beach.

The cashflow can get easy after you have accomplished yourself and have gained many years of experience, but it can be extremely daunting when you have just started out. You might not make any money at all! Sometimes, you have to wait for your payments to come in for months.

So, how do you enjoy being a digital nomad while on the road?

Join a Digital Nomad Community

The more you interact with your kind of people, the better network you will be able to build. You should be part of a digital nomad community to learn from other nomads, know about their challenges and victories, what drives them, and how they cope with productivity issues.

It's also good for getting work recommendations and discovering new opportunities. You may work remotely, but that doesn't mean you don't need to connect with people. Make it a point to connect with like-minded people from all across the globe.

You can find community groups on Facebook, LinkedIn, and also on sites like Meetup and Nomad List.

Plan Your Work Life

Don't go with the flow! That's the wrong approach to anything in life. Be intentional about what you want to do and how you want to do it. Have a work calendar in place. Be specific about your work hours and decide on a workplace. If you are going to be living in a campervan, have a designated place for your work. Make sure you have access to whatever you may need while working—laptop, WiFi connection, headphones, notebook, pen, some inspiring books and quotes on your table, and of course some good coffee.

Take a Break Whenever You Need to

You may want to work every single day of your digital nomad life, but you need to take time off before you feel burnt out. Go on a nature hike, cook an outdoor meal with your friends, or read your favorite book. The idea is to log yourself out of the digital arena and immerse in something real and tangible. When you go back to work after relaxing and renewing your mental strength, you will do even better at your current project.

Keep Honing Your Skills

Never be too satisfied with what you have in terms of skills or knowledge. Always be ready to learn new things, develop new skills and gain as much knowledge as possible. There's so much to observe and learn in the digital realm that it can never get enough. For instance, if you are a blogger, you should follow other blogs and see how other bloggers work and sustain themselves—what are their income streams and what skills they have.

Choose Slow Travel Over Sightseeing

As a digital nomad, it's very important to travel at a slow pace and stick to a place for at least a few weeks if not months. When you pursue working and traveling together, you can't rush through places. You can't have hectic itineraries or indulge in touristic sightseeing. When you arrive in a new place, you need to allow it to unveil itself to you layer by layer with each experience that you take—going for a walk, eating at a local food joint, walking the streets, talking to the locals, and simply observing the sights and sounds.

You may spend a day at your laptop in a cool cafe soaking in the atmosphere, and on another day, you may just relax by the poolside doing nothing at all. Slow travel is not very activity-driven. You need to choose quality over quantity.

Set Your Goals

If you don't set your goals, you may just get lost in whatever you currently have on your plate. Have a clear vision of where you want to see yourself in the next two years or five years and work toward that. For instance, if you want to start your own business and see it thrive in the next two years, have a plan of action in place.

Besides, setting goals keeps you motivated and energetic. It keeps you from stagnating, and you want to give your best each day.

Don't Limit Your Earning Potential

Some digital nomads limit themselves to just one job they have taken. They don't explore other opportunities or experiment with their abilities. If you are a creative thinker, the possibilities are immense. Remember, the more you explore, the more options you will have and more money you will make.

Build Your Social Media Following

Although you don't need to stress over cultivating a huge following on social media, you should be active on at least a couple of channels. The purpose is to connect with more and more people for better work opportunities. For instance, if you stay active on LinkedIn by posting something relevant and interesting regularly and also engage on others' posts, you will get a chance to showcase your skills and experience to a lot of potential clients.

As a digital nomad, you should market yourself well. You should be seen to be approached for work. Keep showcasing your work life, sharing glimpses of your personal life, and reaching out to new people. However, don't be spammy or you will end up annoying people! You shouldn't post too much nor too little about yourself. Observe other successful accounts and see what they post and how they engage with their followers.

Sign up on Websites That Offer Freelance Work

You can find all kinds of freelance work at portals like Upwork, Fiverr, Freelancer, and Behance, just to name a few. Although the freelance gigs on such websites are highly competitive and the pay may not excite you much, they do give you a chance to establish yourself as a digital nomad and build your portfolio.

However, as your portfolio grows and you showcase your skills on social media or on your blog, your potential clients are going to approach you for work, and then you will be in a position to ask for your price.

Outsource Your Work Whenever Required

Some digital nomads make the mistake of doing everything on their own and not designating an appropriate person for a task. For instance, if you are a YouTuber, you don't have to do all the editing work your-self. You can hire somebody to do it for you while you spend those hours planning for your next video.

It's the age of virtual assistants. Take advantage of that and hire an effi-cient individual who could take care of all the jobs that consume a lot of your precious time, which you can utilize for more crucial tasks. You should find an assistant, who can work from anywhere just like you, to assign tasks like replying to professional emails, scheduling social media posts, and researching the latest trends in the specific field you are working in. The key is to find the smartest way to work.

Choose Your Accommodation Carefully

Although you don't need to look for a place to stay while living in an RV, there could be situations or possibilities when you want to check into a hotel or an Airbnb for a few days. As a digital nomad, make an appropriate choice and stay at a place that offers good WiFi connectivity and has a comfortable work atmosphere. You should ideally stay at places that have lots of art and creativity oozing through their walls and corners. Avoid staying at places with no character and charm.

Get a Business License

You may not need to do it immediately as you start your digital nomad life, but you will have to get your business registered at some point. There are different rules as to how much a sole proprietor can earn and at what point they need to pay taxes. You don't have to worry about the business license when you work as a sole proprietor and don't make a huge income. However, it's good to be aware of such things to avoid any sudden penalties from the government.

Sort out Your Client Invoicing

When it comes to raising invoices and getting paid, PayPal is the most commonly used medium. You can key in your bank account details and allow the money to be transferred from your client's PayPal to yours and then finally to your bank account.

You should be aware that PayPal charges a really high processing fee every time you get paid by a client. Perhaps you want to charge your clients keeping the PayPal fees in mind. There are alternative payment mediums like Transferwise Borderless Banking and Payoneer, which are ideal for digital nomads.

Buy a Digital Nomad Insurance

You should purchase low-cost nomad insurance that should offer you both health and travel insurance, trip cancellation benefits, and protect your nomad gear, and you should be able to register online from anywhere.

If you cancel or shorten your travel for a covered reason, you should receive reimbursements for costs like RV rentals and campground reservations.

Cut Down Your Expenses

It's extremely important to reduce your spending as you start your digital nomad life. An RV life has its own set of expenses that you will have to bear. You will be buying groceries as well as paying for the internet and RV insurance, maintenance, and annual charges, and if you have bought the RV on loan then that's going to be an expense for a while. Thus, it's good to live minimalistically and focus on building funds for the future.

Stay Connected to Your People

A digital nomad's life can get quite lonely sometimes. You may find yourself just immersed in work from various remote locations with nobody to talk to. It can be depressing and hard to deal with. To combat that, you should try to keep in touch with your family and old friends. It's good to nurture relationships even though you may not see everyone as regularly as you would like to. Stay connected through technology.

Digital Nomad Mistakes to Avoid

Although digital nomadism is growing quite rapidly these days, not everyone is doing it right. It's a possibility that you might not enjoy it even though you thought it's your passion. There are certain mistakes you should not make while relying on your laptop and internet.

Expecting Too Much Too Soon

As a digital nomad who's living in a campervan, you need to make a lot of new adjustments in your everyday life, and if you are not doing it solo then there might be more changes to adapt to. You can't expect things to be rosy on their own. You will have to make it work.

If you feel you aren't really enjoying it as much as you thought, you need to give it time. It's a huge shift from a conventional life to a life literally on the road. You shouldn't be surprised if eventually you start loving your RV life and find it as normal as your city life.

Depending on Feeling Motivated to Work

You need to have a disciplined approach toward your work every day. Don't wait to feel inspired or motivated. There will be days when you will not feel upbeat. You may rather feel lazy and unhappy for no reason. Try activities like meditation or yoga, but get on your desk and finish the assignment.

You need to train your mind to do the work that needs to be done. Make the most of the morning hours and leave the inconsequential tasks for the latter part of the day.

Not Traveling Enough

Yes, quality is better than quantity, and you don't necessarily have to explore every nook and cranny of a countryside or a town, but you need to travel! Don't make the mistake of overcommitting yourself to work and sidelining travel completely. Remember, your core idea of switching to an RV life is to have freedom to travel. So, create strategies to balance work and travel.

You should keep aside at least two days of your week strictly for exploring places and getting into activities that you enjoy.

Working in Isolation

Some people, especially the digital nomads, like to work in isolation and not mingle with anybody. On the contrary, you should be outgoing and try to build your network. Remember, having a huge network is a strength that you cannot trade for anything. It's the backbone of whatever income you are going to make as a digital entity.

Having No Mental Clarity

If you take up a laptop lifestyle because it looks like an easy option, you have no mental clarity about what you really want to do. You should have clarity on your goals in life—both professional and personal. Don't choose the digital nomad lifestyle because you think it's just about fun and no work.

Choose it for the right reasons—you have the skills, you know how to work remotely, you love your work, and you want to enjoy the flexibility of working from anywhere and traveling at the same time.

Not Exploring New Avenues of Making Money

You may be a great writer, who's successfully blogged for many years. You take great pictures and are pretty comfortable talking in front of the camera as well. Perhaps it's time for you to try vlogging, start your own podcast, or contribute your pictures to a stock photography site.

Focus on your skills and make them a channel of monetization. Don't just stick to one thing and restrict your horizon.

Not Investing in Online Courses and Webinars

Learning has never been easier. In today's age, you can get enrolled in so many different online courses; some of them are even free to join, which is such an advantage. Look for courses and webinars that match your goals and vision. Devote time to learning and broadening your skillset, so that your resume looks stronger.

Not Defining Your Niche

Although it's good to be known for various things, you should specialize in one particular field. If you are an artist, be known for a certain kind of art; if you are a blogger, write about a niche topic; if you are a digital entrepreneur, let your products be unique and point toward something etched out.

For instance, if you aim to be a digital nomad who has an RV as their home, perhaps that should be your niche as a digital content creator.

Not Being Independent and Resourceful

This can be a really foolish mistake on your part: to always rely on something until it dodges you. Have a backup plan of everything—be it food, internet, or electricity. Don't depend on your surroundings or circumstances for your basic needs as a digital nomad. Think of innovative ways to work and travel in different scenarios—for instance, if you have no internet while you need to attend a zoom meeting, you should borrow your neighbor's smartphone with a high internet speed. Your neighbor can be anybody close to you depending on your current location.

Neglecting Your Health

No matter what you pursue in life, keeping your health in check should be your top priority. You cannot wait for a perfect day to start taking care of your body, mind, and soul. You need to nourish it every single day for it to stay healthy. Your health is actually the foundation of everything you do in life—be it your financial goals, your work vision, or your travel dreams, everything depends on how healthy you are.

So, avoid long hours of work without a break, limit your caffeine intake, eat nutritious food, and get into some sort of physical exercise every day.

Digital nomadism is a brilliant concept and fortunately, more and more organizations are being receptive to it. However, it may not be for you if you don't enjoy working on a laptop, connecting with new people, working under pressure sometimes, or are unwilling to learn new skills.

It may look like an easy job, but it's highly demanding and time consuming. You should weigh the pros and cons before you dive in completely, or you can make a slow transition.

CHAPTER 6

HOW TO CREATE PASSIVE INCOME

IN TODAY'S STRESSFUL AND DYNAMIC WORLD, EVERYBODY IS looking for a passive source of cash flow in their lives. Everybody is seeking a way out from the constant struggle that each one of us have to go through every single day. Perhaps passive income is the way out for anyone who's enslaved to working nine to five without any real growth or happiness. Passive income allows you to escape the stressful city life and be anywhere, anytime; live the way you like without any obligations. So, what is passive income and how do we create it?

Most people have this misconception about passive income that it's something you earn for doing nothing. But that's far from the truth. In fact, you do have to work hard at creating passive income, at least the foundation of it, and later you need to maintain it. To create passive income for yourself, you need to first understand its concept and try to relate yourself to it. Passive income is the money you earn without really working actively because you have already worked at something that is generating income for you. After you have identified and accomplished a stream of passive income, you won't have to work at it every day. Nevertheless, you will have to do some work on and off.

For instance, if you rent out your own house to somebody, you don't have to work at generating an income. The house is already there and you have somebody staying there, which earns you an income—that's your passive income or you may also call it an income that you make while sleeping. Yes, you can actually make money while you are not doing anything! However, you will need to make sure that your house is well maintained and that it's occupied by the right kind of people. So yes, there's a certain level of effort from your end but it's technically your passive income.

There are people who never get down to creating passive income for themselves. They continue to slog all their lives because they never really give thought to the idea of passive income. They never really understand their own abilities. Whatever may be the case, you can work toward creating your passive income if you think about it today. Yes, you need to first convince yourself to do it.

You should think of passive income sources to be able to quit your job forever and live a life of freedom. If you haven't created any source of passive cash flow for yourself, you will need to work all your life. So, it's your choice! What do you want to do? You want to create something today that makes you money even when you don't want to work tomorrow or you want to be stuck in your daily grind all your life.

You can produce passive income by creating several assets like buying land, property, or an RV. As a creative individual, you can write books and publish them, put up your paintings on sale, or make YouTube videos and continue to earn from them for years and years to come.

You can think about investing as a foundation of creating passive income—when you put in some money today, it generates significant returns later. However, you need to be really patient and strategic with your investments. You need to first study the market, develop some knowledge, and then choose the right kind of investment options. You also need to have a certain mindset about investing, which is the mindset of growing your wealth slowly over the period of several years and not instantly. Nobody becomes rich in a day. You may want to gamble, but that's not a good idea. Most people make the mistake of treating investing like gambling, forgetting that the two are totally different terms with different outcomes.

Yes, investing does come with a certain level of risk. There are all sorts of investment options available; some are high-risk and medium-risk while some are low-risk. If you are looking for a high return, you need to take high risks, too. So, you need to understand your risk appetite and decide for yourself.

What Is Not Passive Income

Now that you have understood the idea of passive income, let's also understand what's not passive income. Your job is not your passive income. Typically, passive income is not the money that you earn from something you are materially part of, such as the salary you get from a job.

Even a second job that you may take for additional income is not your passive income because you would need to go to work every day to get paid. Non-income producing assets such as non-dividend paying stocks and cryptocurrencies are not passive income. Investing can produce passive income for you, but only if the assets you have pay interest or dividends.

The Idea of Multiple Income Streams

So, how many income streams should you ideally have? Your income streams should depend upon your present financial conditions and your future financial goals. Of course, the more you earn, the better it is for your financial security. However, there are many aspects to consider while you set out to make some extra money. You can't and you shouldn't wear yourself out making money and not savor what you have in the present moment. Besides, you should not lose focus from the main goal of your life.

Although it's a good idea to generate income from rental properties, business ventures, and dividends apart from your regular earned income, you need to strike a healthy balance between your efforts to make passive income and making the best use of your time.

You may see others making money in a certain way quite successfully; however, it's not necessary that the same idea or pattern of working is going to work for you, too. You need to consider your own skills, expertise, and lifestyle. You need to be aware of your circumstances, how much you will be able to commit, and be ready to make some sacrifices for your long-term growth.

Why You Should Create a Passive Income

Before you find ways to create a passive income, you should be convinced that it's important. There are many benefits of a passive income. It's not something that you should pursue just for the sake of it. You should have a goal behind making a passive income. Everything you do in life should be goal-driven, then the results are more meaningful and long-lasting.

Your passive income is important because it gives you the time you need to garner various experiences in life. Your active income takes away all your time. You are barely able to meet all your needs and obligations. You simply wait for the right time or enough money to do the things that you really like. Time is more valuable than money. You can lose money and still earn it back, but if you lose time, it can never be recovered. Most of us spend all our days just working from morning till evening; some of us even work long hours and also over the weekends. Time keeps slipping away, and at the end of every year, we feel that time simply flies and we haven't been able to accomplish much. That's why a passive income is necessary. With passive income flowing, you will not have to worry about actively working to make your ends meet. You will have all the time to do the things you always wanted to do—jog, swim, cook, meet friends and family, travel, sketch, paint, write, or learn a new sport.

Passive income gives you freedom to utilize your time the way you want. You don't spend all your hours just working and worrying about your future. If you have enough passive income for yourself, it's going to help you look at your future with confidence. You will not feel anxious or stressed about unforeseen circumstances or financial instability. You will not have a fear of losing your job because you know you have sufficient funds to sustain yourself for a long time.

The best part is that you don't have to live with limitations. When you are stuck in a nine-to-five job, you can't go on holidays whenever you want. You will need to ask your boss for every little thing. You will have to be at your desk to be able to prove your productivity. Even during the pandemic when people have been working from home, they are glued to their desks most of the time. The work stress is still the same for a full-time employee of a company. On the other hand, when you have a passive income to support you, there's no need for you to be at your desk all the time, ask for somebody's permission to go on a vacation, meet a deadline or targets, or slog for hours and hours every day. In fact, it gives you the freedom to work from anywhere and at your own pace. You can travel to any place and stay there for as long as you want.

Passive income is vital to your mental health and peace. It gives you stability, growth, and also the ability to help others in need. Therefore, you should try different streams and find a way or two that could generate passive profit for you.

Passive Income Streams You Can Explore

Earn Dividends

You can make some extra money by investing in companies that pay dividends to their shareholders. Dividends are profits that companies make, and since you have purchased their shares, you also are eligible to partake in the profit. The dividend rate is determined by the board of directors of the company—it's like the more shares you buy of a company, the more dividends you earn. Let's say for example, if a company announces a quarterly dividend of $0.60 per share and if you own 150 shares of stock, you will receive $90 for that quarter.

However, it's not necessary that companies always pay dividends to their shareholders. Sometimes they also choose to reinvest the profit in the business—they might want to expand the company, share repurchases, or pay off debts. Additionally, you should be aware that companies may suffer losses and may pay out a very small amount of dividend or may not be able to pay out any dividends at all. To increase your chances of receiving high dividend returns, invest in dividend aristocrats or preferred stocks.

Invest in Real Estate

Although your investments are driven by market volatility, you can choose some of the old ways to invest and see your money grow. The best form of passive income is owning real estate. Although it's not so simple to purchase a house or land, it's definitely one of the best investments you can ever make. The real estate value grows with time, which assures a meaningful return over the years. Yes, you will have to deal with expenses like maintenance and repair, which is in addition to the purchase price of the property. As long as you are ready to bear the costs involved in acquiring your own land or house, it can prove to be a source of revenue for you in the long run.

Another way to extract profit out of real estate is by investing in real estate investment trusts (REITs). What are REITs? They allow you to invest in real estate assets just like you invest in other industries—by buying individual company stocks, mutual funds, or exchange traded funds (ETF). Now, the good part is that as a stockholder of a REIT, you can secure a share of the revenue earned without going through the headache of actually buying, managing, or financing a property.

Asset Sharing

You can also generate some passive income through the assets you own by leasing or renting them to whoever is in need. For instance, you can rent out an extra space in your property—it could be your backyard or garage. You can sign up on platforms like HomeCamper and JustPark that allow you to lease land to people looking to park an RV in your premises.

There are various options when it comes to renting out your house—you can rent out a spare portion or even one single bedroom to someone who may need it. You can also list your home on Airbnb for travelers. Not just your house, but you can even rent out your car via platforms like Turo or Getaround and also your bike on a platform like Spinlister.

INVEST IN MUTUAL Funds

Mutual funds are also a great way to invest your funds for future use. And they are a lot less riskier than buying direct company stocks. As a mutual fund investor, you participate in the fund's total holdings, which means all the profits and losses are yours, too. Mutual funds are managed by professional fund managers on your behalf; thus, you don't have to be worried about market fluctuations much. Since a mutual fund has a diversified portfolio, there are stocks of multiple companies under one fund and your risk of losing money is also distributed.

Mutual funds investments should be aimed at long-term growth and not quick gains, as the market doesn't work that way. You are highly likely to make profit if you stay invested for a long period of time, at least three to five years, despite market volatility.

Certificate of Deposit or Savings Account

You can make some passive income by putting in some money in a high-return certificate of deposit (CD) or savings account via an online bank, which offers you the best interest rate available. The first thing you should do is to look out for the best CD rates in the country and invest in it. And, if your financial institution is supported by the FDIC, you will secure a guaranteed yield of principal, which is approximately $250,000.

The returns on CDs and savings accounts are usually not too high and they are unable to match the inflation rate; nevertheless, they are far better than keeping your money in your checking account where you see no growth at all.

Bond Laddering

As the name suggests, a bond ladder is your money growing in different stages—you buy multiple bonds that have various maturity dates. This way you can generate predictable income, stay invested, and avoid some potential risks of fluctuating interest rates. Thus, it's a favorite with retirees and people who want to generate some passive income over the period of several years.

It's always wise to buy multiple bonds to distribute your risk and remove the risk of any one particular bond affecting your complete portfolio. If overall interest rates increase, it could reduce the value of your bonds, which is why many investors choose bond ETFs, which give you a diversified fund of bonds that eliminates the risk of one particular bond bringing down your returns.

Own a Vending Machine

You can own a vending machine and make some side passive income for yourself. Whether you are a new or an experienced entrepreneur, a vending machine business is quite profitable and versatile. It doesn't really demand a very high-cost startup. Yes, you will need a location and maybe $2,000 or more to buy a vending machine. After that, it's just refilling and servicing your machines, which you can outsource as well. You will lose some of the profits, though.

Buy and Sell Domain Names

You can also make money by buying domain names and reselling them later when their value increases. It's called domain investing or domaining, which is kind of a stock trading. A few things you need to keep in mind while purchasing a domain name is that it's a proper noun because if you use any word randomly, you might not find buyers for it later. People buy domain names that are relevant to their business. For instance, a person may need a domain name like NewYork.com if they plan to launch a website that has all information about New York city. Also, .com domains are usually sold at a higher price across the U.S.

Perhaps you can start with buying a domain name for as low as $10 in the beginning and wait for its price to grow. However, if it doesn't increase, you will lose your money invested and then there's an annual fee that you will have to pay.

Create Digital Products

You can create passive income by building certain assets, such as digital products, photo licensing, and affiliate sales. For instance, you can write an eBook once and then continue to earn an income out of it. You may want to invest some time or money in its marketing, or you may follow the passive approach and let it find its audience on its own. Just like eBooks, you can continue to earn passive income through your blog, YouTube videos, online courses, or mobile apps.

If you have a flair for photography, you can license your pictures to stock image websites like ShutterStock, Adobe Stock, and Alamy. You get instant exposure by uploading your pictures on such sites, as they are accessed by so many different people from across the globe. While the site takes a certain percentage as their commission, you get most of it in your bank account.

Affiliate Sales

Affiliate marketing is one of the favorite ways of generating some passive cash flow for digital content creators. When somebody buys a product or a service via an affiliate link, which you have embedded in your website, you earn a small commission at no extra cost to your blog visitor. You can place affiliate links not just on your blog but also on a podcast or a video. They usually pay you a fixed rate or a percentage of the cost of the product or service sold.

So, you can choose affiliate links according to your niche and the kind of content you create on your blog or channel. Affiliate marketing works when you create high-quality, relevant content on a consistent basis. However, it's not wise to place affiliate marketing links of too many brands. Just stick to two or three at a time and see how it works. Content creators of all kinds make a huge amount of money (somewhere between $1k to $100k a month) with affiliate marketing alone, which proves that it's a great passive income tool.

Go for a Limited Business Partnership

You can join hands with an entrepreneur without investing any of your time, energy, or expertise in the business. You can simply make your financial contribution to the company and allow your partner to take all decisions and deal with everyday operations.

As the company earns profit, you take a certain percentage as your share, which will be supported by a percentage proprietorship of the company.

Yes, of course, you should be comfortable investing in a partnership like that. You can also look for such business partnerships online.

Create Your own App

It's the age of apps! So, if you can come up with a solution to a task or an easy way of doing something, you can create your own app and help others. You will be investing your thinking abilities, time, effort, or money just once and it will reward you for a long time. Your app should be able to help mobile users perform certain difficult jobs with ease, such as editing videos and photos, ordering food, booking a ticket, making a transaction, learning yoga, and all sorts of things. As soon as your app is ready to use, anybody can download it and that's how you make money.

There are apps that are free to download and then there are apps that charge a nominal fee. You also have the option of running in-app ads to make your users pay. However, to keep the cash coming, you will need to keep your app upgraded by keeping it relevant and adding better features.

Additionally, you will need to ensure that the data your app gathers complies with privacy laws, which vary from nation to nation.

Sell Your Designs Online

If you are creative and art is your thing, you can make your own designs for various products like water bottles, phone covers, coffee mugs, t-shirts, and others, and upload them on print-on-demand platforms like Redbubble, CafePress, Zazzle, and Teespring. So, every time someone purchases a product that has your design on it, you will make money. The best part is that you don't have to deal with storage, printing, or shipping, as it's completely digital.

Write eBooks

You can write books and continue to earn royalties. However, publishing a book is a headache of its own, which you can avoid by investing your time in writing a digital book, which is an eBook. It requires absolutely no financial investment from your end. You don't have to look out for publishers. You can self-publish an eBook on Amazon and get readers from all across the world. All you need is a good subject to write on, a flair for writing, and some research skills. You might want to invest in an editor to critique your content and a designer to give it a good cover. However, you can get those jobs done at affordable rates.

The real challenge comes when you need to get down to marketing your eBook, which is extremely hard. Of course, if you have a popular blog or social media presence, you can get some views quickly, and it may help in creating a pre-release hype. But then you need to be innovative, be persistent, and reach out to people to get some sales happening.

Also, you need to be writing your next eBook instead of stressing over the promotion of the current one. Do some market research and try to understand what topics people are searching and write eBooks on those subjects. The more you create, the better you get at the job and the more chances you have of creating revenue out of it.

Rent out Household Stuff

You may not want to rent out anything and everything that you have in your house. But you can list out items that are not going to be of any use to you while you will be living in a motorhome, such as lawnmowers, coolers, instruments, a bike or motorcycle, and also your car. Make an inventory of items that people typically like to take on rent and put them all together in a place where your potential customers may discover them and take whatever they need.

You can start with small items and then as you see people's interest in certain items, you can add more items to your inventory. You can continue to rent out household items even after you have moved to RV living and keep it as a side business.

Use Your Car for Advertisements

If you are fond of driving some extra miles, you can perhaps approach an advertising agency who might want to use your car as a platform for promotions at no additional cost to you. It may be a little unique and flashy way of making some extra bucks, but it doesn't really require much effort from your end. All you have to do is drive through the town, which you do anyway. The agency will review your driving patterns—the places you drive to every day and the miles you typically cover. If your driving proclivity is in line with an advertiser, the agency will paint your vehicle with the ads, and you start making money! It will be easier for you to get the deal if your car looks new and you have a good driving record.

Using your car for advertisements can be a good way of earning extra income while you are still planning your exit from corporate life. You can keep the extra cash made here for future use while you will be living on wheels.

Once you create something of value, it can fetch you passive income all your life. So, whether it's a property that you buy today or a product you create, it can become a source of cash flow for you later in life. Therefore, it's always good to keep experimenting with your capabilities, learn new skills, and network so that you can make most of what you have and monetize your assets whenever there's a need.

MAXIMIZE YOUR PASSIVE INCOME

It's great to produce a few streams of passive income for yourself; however, it's even better to let it grow and become more profitable as time goes by. So, after you have accomplished a passive income source that suits your priorities, lifestyle, and expertise, you should think of ways to maximize it and not keep that extra cash idle.

Reinvest Your Passive Earnings in a High-Yield Account

You should put your passive income into a high-interest paying bank and let it continue to grow. Does that sound too good to be true? Yes, you can do that! Believe it or not, your money grows exponentially after a point. So, give it time to come to that point. Passive income doesn't mean you have got money to squander. You need to have a conscious and a responsible approach even toward your passive income. It's your hard-earned income!

Reinvest in Real Estate if it Works for You

If something works for you, reinvest some of your passive money back into it to make it grow more. For instance, you may boost your investment by buying another property from the money that you have earned from a rental property. If real estate works for you, keep reinvesting in it to gain more profits.

Do More of What Works for You

In another scenario, if you see growth in your income by selling digital products or through affiliate marketing, continue to grow your passive income by those sources—create more digital products, collaborate more, or write SEO blogs to draw more relevant readership and encourage more affiliate sales. The idea is to do more of what works for you to gain maximum profit.

Save Tax on Your Passive Income

You should be aware that passive income is taxable. Thus, you should also think of ways to protect your passive earnings from high taxation. You should be aware of how your passive income is taxed. For instance, income generated from renting a property is taxed differently from trade activities and business earnings. Understanding taxation related to various forms of income can be overwhelming; thus, you may want to reach out to a professional to analyze your tax situation. They can guide you on recordkeeping and the documents required during a return filing.

You should also understand that the Internal Revenue Service (IRS) has a particular guideline as to what kind of income is considered as material participation, which defines whether a taxpayer has earned an active income or a passive income.

To save on taxes, it's important that you ensure your passive earnings qualify for long-term capital gains treatment. A long-term capital gain is when you sell an asset held for more than a year.

Additionally, you can purchase municipal bonds from your state and avoid paying any income taxes. You can also consider Saver's Credit to reduce your tax liability, as it offers a special tax break to people who fall under the low to moderate income bracket and want to set aside income for retirement. When you use the passive income toward a tax-advantaged account, it can add to your ability of not paying any taxes.

Passive income isn't something you can start generating in a day. It takes time. You need patience, understanding of the market, and lots of resourcefulness and research to be able to create it over the period of time. Additionally, it's important to manage your passive income smartly to be able to retain it and make it grow even more. Keep your expenses in check, invest wisely, and refrain from doing something that doesn't work for you.

CHAPTER 7

DEBUNKED MYTHS ABOUT PASSIVE INCOME

DON'T LIVE BY MYTHS AND LEGENDS. LIVE BY TRUTH. PEOPLE have developed so many false notions about passive income that it can be scary! The more knowledge you have of various ways of creating passive income and growing your money, the better off you will be in terms of your personal finances. Most of us never achieve our financial goals because of the many myths and misconceptions we live with. We find the stock market too scary to try. We want to stick to the old, traditional ways of protecting our money. We fail to experiment, learn, and grow.

It's time we debunked some of the deadly myths associated with passive income. To begin with, each penny that you make is the outcome of some level of investment from your end. So, whether it's active or passive income, it's the result of some sort of work that you put in. There have always been people who have had passive income. It's not really a new phenomenon. It's just that digital media has blown it out of proportion because a lot of people in today's age have chosen to take the unconventional path of quitting their jobs, adapting to digital nomadism, and living in a campervan. So yes, passive income is perhaps the need of the hour.

It's good to have passive income. As covered in the last chapter, passive income takes away a lot of stress from your life. It gives you financial freedom and more confidence to face the future. But how do you get to a point where you actually start enjoying the rewards of your hard work? How do you make passive income when you are surrounded by so many myths about it?

The first step to keep myths at bay in your life is to stop any wrong advice from settling in your head. You will be told to do different things and advised to not do certain things; however, you should use your own thinking ability and your own research skills before you take any financial decision in your life—be it big or small. You need to understand that people advise you from their own understanding, knowledge, and experience, which may not always be right.

So, leave behind the misconceptions and understand the true value of passive income. Align the right strategies of passive earnings with your life.

Let's dive into the myths about passive income that most people live with:

Passive Income Is Something Elusive

Many people believe that passive income is something that's hard to achieve, which is why they never really take steps toward building it. They find it too far-fetched, which keeps them from learning, exploring, and making money. On the contrary, passive income is one of the most basic concepts of personal finances. Everybody should be able to create at least one income stream for themselves, which is passive in nature—something they don't have to actively work at every day.

For instance, you can create passive income by doing something as simple as leasing out your farmland for recreational activities. If you think about it, there are many options to generate income without really "working." It's all about analyzing the available resources and how they can be optimized. Passive income is something as natural as an active income—it's just that the former is earned for the future.

You Don't Have to Move a Finger

If you think passive income is as easy as not doing anything at all, you are in for some serious enlightening. Yes, of course, you don't have to go to work every day like you do in a conventional job, but you are supposed to upgrade, reinvent, and maintain the source of your passive cash flow from time to time. For instance, if you make a lot of money through your YouTube channel—through affiliate commissions and ad clicks, you do need to make sure that your videos are up to date and relevant even if they have received millions or billions of views. If there's anything you feel needs to be added in the video to make it more valuable or if there's anything that needs to be edited because it's not relevant anymore, you need to do it.

Similarly, if you generate passive income through writing eBooks, you will need to keep working at their marketing. Nobody is bothered to check out your eBooks just like that. No matter how famous you are as a writer, you still need to promote your work to intrigue people to check it out. Additionally, you have to come up with different marketing strategies, think out of the box, and network with a lot of relevant people to reach your audience.

Even affiliate marketing is not as simple as it may sound. It's not just about inserting affiliate links somewhere in your content for people to click through and make a purchase as you get your sweet commission.

You are supposed to be strategic about your content for it to make people click on those affiliate links.

Any digital passive income has to be maintained with constant hard work, an innovative approach, creativity, and research.

Real Estate Is All You Need

Owning a land or property is definitely one of the best investments you can ever make, but it comes with its own flaws and troubles. You can't predict if property rates will go up or remain stagnant. Additionally, there are quite a few dreaded property related issues, such as nasty tenants, delayed rent payments, and property disputes.

Yes, you should invest in real estate, but only when you are aware of its pros and cons. When you invest in real estate, you need to do a lot of hard work—both physically and mentally. You need to find a good real estate agent, see different properties, analyze various things, arrange for a loan, go through different documents, and get into a lot of legalities to finally own a piece of land. Not everybody has the temperament to undergo so much hassle. Not to mention, you need to have a hefty sum of money to make the initial down payment. So, it is a lot of work!

After you have purchased a property, you might want to make some changes and improvements in it, which involves a whole lot of expenses. If you choose to rent out the property, there's another set of legalities you will need to follow. And let's not forget expenses like paying for the maintenance, parking charges, etc.

Not many people pay attention to the fact that when you pay back your home loan, the payment initially goes toward the interest amount first and then toward the principal amount. Thus, you end up paying a lot more than the actual cost of the property. If you choose to pay back your loan over a period of 25 to 30 years at a changing interest rate, it's going to cost you a lot.

Buying a property is beneficial only when you are prepared to pay off your debt fast, maybe over a period of 10 years at a fixed interest rate. You might have to pay large chunks of your loan initially to begin paying the principal amount quickly. Your property will become a source of your passive earnings only when your debt is paid in full and when your earnings are way more than your maintenance costs.

You Can Literally Sleep

Although you can relax by the poolside in a swanky resort with your passive income rolling in, you will still need to constantly work at making sure that it keeps coming. You will need to analyze any of the passive sources of income, online or offline; each one of them has its own set of requirements to be fulfilled from time to time. For instance, even if you put your money in a high-yield savings account so that your money grows over time, you will still need to keep an eye on your savings—whether it's worth your efforts or not. Sometimes, people are unable to deposit a large amount of money in their savings account, which leads to low savings, too. The trick is to leave large amounts of funds in maybe multiple accounts for a really long time for you to use it as a passive income later.

Thus, you don't really sleep while enjoying your passive income. You need to monitor your income, savings, and investments regularly to keep all of them intact.

It's Easy to Create Passive Income

People usually have a very imbalanced perception of creating passive income. Some people think it's too hard to create passive income and they never work toward it, while some people assume it's too easy. In today's digital age, there are people who have created passive earnings through YouTube videos, blogs, social media, online courses, eBooks, and podcasts. However, none of the jobs are easy in any manner. You need to start from scratch and build your authority by placing one brick at a time. There's no shortcut to income generation. You need to devote a certain number of hours every day, sacrificing a lot of fun things, like going out or lazing around on weekends, for the sake of creating quality content and building an audience.

You Become Rich by Investing in Stocks

Some people believe in getting rich fast and the stock market is their favorite place to be. Although buying stocks can be a great investment model, it might not be everyone's cup of tea. Assuming that investing in the stock market will make you rich is not right. Yes, of course, you can grow your wealth by stock market investments, but there's a lot of study, research, and understanding required to be able to do that. You don't make profit by following someone's advice or simply investing because you feel the stock is going to perform well.

While there have been people who have gained enormous wealth by stock market investments, there have also been people who have lost a lot of their precious money. So, the stock market is extremely dicey and unpredictable. It's one of the riskiest investment options; therefore, if you choose to grow your money through the stock market, you should do it only after studying the market trends, doing a fundamental analysis of various companies, and investing at the right time.

Also, it's important to have a long-term view of your wealth. You can generate passive income by investing in stocks; however, that happens only with a proper plan and strategy.

ONE SOURCE OF REVENUE IS ENOUGH

This can be lethal. If you rely on just one single source of income, you are highly unlikely to become rich. The basic idea of passive wealth is having multiple revenue streams. If you have invested money in a property and that property's value fades away in the shadow of other better properties, you should think of ways to tackle that. A property with depreciating value becomes a liability. To avoid getting in a situation like that, you need to diversify your investment portfolio and sow your "passive income" seeds at multiple places.

You may consider buying more than one property so that if one doesn't give you value, you can pin your hopes on the other. Of course, it's not so easy to purchase or own multiple properties, but you should make a quick decision about selling off a not-so-nifty property and switching to another.

It's important to keep looking for different investment options—the stock market, savings account, digital assets, real estate, and renting out your house. The more options you have in terms of investments, the better financial health you will be in.

PURPOSELESS WEALTH CREATION

If you create passive income without an end goal in mind, it's not going to be sustainable. Each of your investments or savings should have a specific purpose for it to be meaningful in the long run. If you invest without a goal, you will not know when to exit the investment or how to make it more profitable. For instance, if you buy stocks or land with a clear goal of reselling it as soon as their value appreciates, you will be able to accomplish it. You should never be aimless or clueless as to what to do with your investments. If you don't exit an investment at the right time, you will end up losing the earned profit.

Your passive income should be able to meet your financial goals. You shouldn't just make money for the sake of it. Purposeful investing helps you make timely financial decisions that save you from losses and enhance your profits.

Wanting Passive Income Is Being Greedy

Yes, you may feel like you are being greedy when you are putting in all your efforts into creating passive income. You can make money from a regular job, be able to meet all your needs, and simply be happy all your life. There's no need to dream of a blue sky, rainbows, and dewdrops on the grass. You can live an ordinary life with little or no adventure in it. With passive earnings, you can choose to be your own boss and pursue the things that make you truly happy.

It's not really satisfying in the long run to travel on a shoestring budget and write about your journeys on your blog. You should rather be talking about creating wealth while experiencing the most wonderful of adventures on the road.

If the wrong notion of "being greedy" is stopping you from making passive wealth for yourself, shrug that thought off. You will limit your own capabilities by submitting to misleading thought patterns and ideas.

Doing Anything Is Fine

You should refrain from doing anything that doesn't make you happy or you have no experience in. Think long-term and let your passive income streams be the pursuits that you are comfortable with. For instance, if you start a blog or a YouTube channel just because that's what is popular, you will soon lose your sheen, and eventually it's not going to be profitable. Whatever you do, it should inspire you and keep you mentally energized. When you pursue something enthusiastically and confidently, it's more rewarding and you will want to stick to it for a long time. On the other hand, if you do something half-baked or quit early, it's not going to give you anything in the long run.

So, before you begin creating passive income for yourself, make a list of your skills and strengths. Pick up avenues that match your professional experiences, interests, passions, and desires so that you can give your best.

You Can Make Passive Income Quickly

Some people live with this fantasy that it's quick to generate some passive earnings. Contrary to such a belief, it takes time to build passive wealth. You need to be patient while working on your passive income. You need to invest your time, skills, mental aptitude, and some money to create some sort of passive income for your retirement or for the life that you want to live with fewer responsibilities.

Remember, passive income is primarily the outcome of your investment of time; thus, you need to have patience and not think of quick ways to make money. Honestly, there is no quick way to create long-term wealth.

You Can Create Passive Wealth Without an Active Income

If there's no active income, there's no possible passive income either. You need to have some money to start with. You need to work at something actively to get to a point of not working. You can't be passive right from the start. If you want to rent out an additional house, you need to work to be able to have sufficient funds to afford an additional house in the first place, right? If you are able to make affiliate sales through your blog, you must have invested in your blog at some point—bought a domain name, a hosting plan, hired a web developer, etc. So, there's always some monetary investment before the evolution of a passive income.

You Can Build a Passive Income Without a Network

Think of any stream of passive earnings, it's built on the foundation of a network. People should know you for something you do. Whether you are a blogger, author, painter, designer, or a YouTuber, you should have an audience to be able to generate some sort of passive cash flow. For instance, if you want to sell your online course or an eBook, you need an audience to consume it.

You need to have a killer network not just to sell your digital products but also to make money through offline ventures. For instance, if you want to give a room in your house to Airbnb, you need to know people to spread the word. Whether it's renting out your property or starting a new business, you need to connect with the right kind of people. If you don't let people know what you have, it's going to be the best kept secret, which nobody is going to find out on their own.

Passive Income Is for the Retirees

Many people keep themselves from exploring various channels of passive earnings thinking that it's only for the retirement life and they are too young to plan it yet. On the contrary, you should start planning your passive income as early as possible. There's no right or wrong age for planning your future. You should think from a broad perspective and be financially innovative as soon as you start working. In fact, the earlier you start, the better it is because you will have ample time to explore, experiment, make mistakes, and recover. If you start late, maybe at the age of 40, you will not have the ability to take many risks. You will want to play it safe and not be too aggressive with your investments.

You Don't Need Experts' Advice

It's okay to follow your own understanding and wisdom, but expert advice is always valuable. You should be willing to learn from others. For instance, if you want to invest in real estate, you need to talk to somebody who has bought properties in the past, somebody who has a market understanding and has knowledge about all the practical and legal stuff related to buying a property.

Don't ever believe that you know it all. When you set out to create a passive earning stream for yourself, you need to learn a lot of things from financial advisors to be able to make wise decisions and strike smarter deals.

That being said, always apply your own wisdom when it comes to making final decisions about anything.

It's Okay Not to Keep a Record of Your Passive Earnings

Most people take their passive earnings for granted or keep no track of it, which is absolutely wrong. It's like wasting your own efforts. When you keep a track of your passive income, you will be able to boost it by doing more of what works and measuring your progress. If something doesn't work or adds no significant value to your overall financial status, you should eliminate it. For instance, if a property's rate hasn't risen for a long time and you see no improvement in sight, you should make a note of it and decide what you want to do next.

It's Okay to Ignore the Expenses

You need to measure up your expenses toward your passive income with the profits made. If your profits are less than the expenses you have made toward building an income, it's not really a fruitful investment. You should make more money than you spend. For instance, if you have invested in expensive camera gear to shoot your YouTube videos, they should generate a significant revenue for you to justify your investment.

You should not only keep track of your expenses but also of your time. If an activity takes too much of your time and doesn't reward you monetarily, you shouldn't be doing it. For instance, if you have spent hours and hours recording podcasts that nobody cares about, you should use your time more wisely.

So, passive income is a serious ball game. There are various facets to it, which you need to understand and live by. Passive returns need to be managed properly in order for them to be sustained. You need to plan your passive income streams, be organized about them, and do the required research. Building passive wealth is a lot of work initially, especially when there's no growth in sight. That's when you need to be patient and keep at it. The exponential growth happens only after a long time.

CHAPTER 8

BENEFITS OF LIVING IN AN RV

As we discussed some of the challenges of living in an RV earlier in the book, now let's also look into some of the amazing benefits of an RV life. The first and foremost thing to love about an RV life is what we have been stressing on throughout the book: the freedom you feel each day as you wake up, go about your business, witness different landscapes and sceneries, and bump into various lovely people. It's an alternative way to live, which is full of excitement every day. Monotony is thrown out of the window. Yes, you do have problems every once in a while, but you are able to deal with them because you have a lot of better things to experience—being in the midst of nature, experiencing serendipity, and doing things that truly make you happy.

The key is to live under no obligation and not to chase things that make no sense in the long run. Money is important to each person's survival. But you don't want to live just to survive, do you? You want to live to experience life—the thousand different beautiful joys. Travel, adventure, and experiencing nature are some of the most valuable aspects of life, not just because they elevate your spirits but also because they make you a better individual. When you travel and learn to meet your ends every day, you become a wiser, more confident, and an independent individual. You learn to tackle every small and big issue of life. Being on the road isn't just "fun" as most of us perceive it, but it's a much deeper experience that adds a lot of meaning and value to one's life.

So, there's a lot to embrace about a motorhome life. If you are jittery about adapting to an RV lifestyle, you should consider the many benefits of living on wheels.

You Breathe in Fresh Air Almost all the Time

Contrary to your city life, living in an RV means living an outdoorsy life, which involves taking in the sunshine, rolling on the grass, and being enveloped by the infinite beauty of the sky. While in your conventional life, you need to try hard to squeeze time for some outdoor activity like running, playing, or simply sitting in the sun; your campervan life allows you to have an abundance of fresh air without even thinking about it. That's a valuable benefit if you think of it not just from your mental and emotional health perspective but also from your physical health point of view.

The more indoor life you live, the more dependent you are on your gadgets, which leads to all sorts of health issues.

YOU LIVE CLOSE TO NATURE

There's simply no better way to get close to nature than experiencing it through a campervan. You can stop by anywhere you want. It's the spontaneity of an RV life that helps you experience nature in the most intimate way possible. You can go for a hike anywhere you like, bathe in the river, sit by a gurgling waterfall, or simply sit to gaze at the mountains.

The good part is that you can always find time to be with nature—whether you have a job or not. For instance, if you are working as a park ranger at a national park, you can be on your job and still experience the rawness of nature around you.

YOU PAY LESS FOR AN RV THAN A PHYSICAL HOUSE

It's a no-brainer! No matter how expensive a brand-new RV is, it's not going to cost you as much as a piece of land or a house. You pay quite an exorbitant amount to own a house, while owning an RV isn't so hard on your pocket. In addition, there are so many other expenses of owning or even renting a house—repair and maintenance work, various household and utility expenses, house taxes, and mortgage payments.

On the other hand, if you choose to rent an RV, it's going to cost you around $100 or so per month, and even if you buy an RV, you can manage it easily with a personal loan. You can do the math and come up with your own conclusion as to what is better.

YOU HAVE FEWER TRAVEL EXPENSES

Travel is usually very expensive, as there are multiple things you need to spend money on, such as air tickets, local public transport, hotels, restaurants, sightseeing, activities, tipping, and so on. However, with an RV, you can easily cut down on a lot of such expenses. For instance, you don't need to spend on transport because your RV is your commute. Then, you don't need to spend on accommodation, as you have a sleep and shower facility in your campervan.

You might want to spend on sightseeing and food once in a while, but that's not a necessity at all.

YOU HAVE FLEXIBILITY IN TERMS OF WORK AND TRAVEL

There's no defined way of doing things in an RV way of life. You have great flexibility in regards to how much you want to work and how much you want to travel. You can choose your own working hours depending on the kind of job you have taken. You can work incessantly for weeks and then take a complete break from work or you can work through the week and relax on the weekends, like the way you typically do.

You are your own boss when it comes to choosing when and how much to work. You may also choose to work for straight six months and set out to explore places in the next six months. The anticipation of travel is what keeps you motivated and energized at work.

YOU MEET SOME AMAZING PEOPLE

The icing on the cake is you get to meet so many amazing people along the way. Yes, of course, you meet different people in your regular life also; however, there's a difference. The people you meet in your corporate life or through your regular social circle have a certain perception of you. They have an opinion about you—they judge for each little thing you do. And, to be honest, they barely give you a chance to be your real self. Most of the time you are pretending to be who they like you to be rather than who you really are.

Fortunately, people who you come across on the road have no preconceived notions about you. They don't judge you, no matter what you do or not do. They accept you the way you are—you can strike great conversations with them, be honest, laugh out loud, and feel more alive at the end of it.

You Become Smarter and Wiser

Since you need to make so many decisions on a daily basis, you become a smarter individual. You learn to become resourceful, work things out in any given scenario, and deal with challenges every day. You learn the value of money, understand the idea of minimalism, and adapt to a healthier lifestyle.

You don't just buy things out of impulse. You learn to spend money wisely and make the most of whatever resources you have.

When a person lives a normal life of going to work every day, catching up with their colleagues, watching movies, shopping, and eating out, they don't really realize what they are doing. They simply do the things that everybody else around is doing, which is why they don't grow as an individual.

You Are Clear About Your Priorities and Goals

The best part is that you think about your goals every single day as you wake up. Your priorities stare at you and make you do the things that make each moment worth living. You don't just wait for the day to get over so that you can fall back on Netflix and retire for the day. When every day is so full of beauty and adventure, you embrace it wholeheartedly. The reason for your happiness is not a promotion, a raise in your salary, or a new partner; the reason for your happiness is you—what you are doing with your life.

You Can Choose Your Travel Experiences

When you travel by plane, train, or bus, you need to operate according to their schedules. Also, these days, it's stressful to travel with so many people due to the pandemic. Even checking into a hotel is not as safe as it used to be. Additionally, you have to choose your travel activities based on what the place has to offer or what your host wants to suggest to you. However, you can do whatever you like anytime while traveling in an RV. You are in the driver's seat; thus, you can plan your own itinerary and even make impromptu additions as per your mood.

You Can Grow Fonder of Your Spouse/Family

RV travel and life can strengthen your relationships. Depending on who you are RVing with—your spouse, partner, friend, or family, you can make your bond sweeter with them. Although an RV doesn't give you much space inside and you might have to be together all the time, it does make you appreciate and respect each other a lot more. There are so many opportunities and situations where you will work as a couple or a family—cooking, eating, traveling, cleaning, and dealing with a hitch or two. In addition, you will find the time to spend some quality moments together, laugh, share experiences and perspectives, and savor the togetherness, not to mention you will be doing a lot of travel activities together, such as exploring, hiking, scuba diving, swimming, camping, watching sunsets, and maybe sleeping under the stars.

You Will Learn Something Every Day

Needless to say, an RV life teaches you something valuable every day. Since it's not a normal life where you do the expected things and have little room for surprises, a motorhome life keeps you on your toes all the time. You learn as you solve a problem, overcome a circumstance, or choose to be resilient in a difficult situation.

In addition, you also get plenty of opportunities to educate yourself about various fields—you get to work at different locations, gain hands-on experience of various jobs, and meet people from different professional backgrounds. Can you even imagine gaining so much experience and education for free in your traditional life?

YOU CAN WORK FROM ANYWHERE

An RV life allows you to work from wherever you like—be it your motorhome living area or the riverside, you can literally make your office anywhere provided you get access to the internet. If you like the view, you can park your RV for a few hours and enjoy working while looking at the white mountains intermittently. Not to mention, a beautiful work location enhances your creativity, boosts your thinking ability, and gives you better focus.

Sitting under a tree with your laptop isn't a fantasy. You can make it happen by just sorting out your life priorities and doing what makes you happy.

YOU LIVE A HAPPIER LIFE

When you live in a motorhome, you have fewer responsibilities and liabilities to deal with. Thus, you live a carefree life. Some people may think of it as a reckless life. However, that's far from the truth. You live a responsible life with all the safety measures in place, and of course, you abide by all the regulations and laws. A carefree and happy life doesn't mean a life devoid of problems and challenges. In fact, there are quite a few issues to deal with almost every day—sometimes you will have connectivity issues while at other times you will fall short of groceries. Nevertheless, the joy and satisfaction of living each day with new expectations and excitement is unparalleled.

An RV life isn't just about whims and fancies. It's chosen by some of the most adventurous of souls who dare to make something different of their lives. Think of the benefits more than the flaws of a motorhome living; that's going to give you the courage to take the leap and be different.

CHAPTER 9

HOW TO AVOID LAW TROUBLES

LIVING IN AN RV ISN'T A NORMAL WAY OF LIFE; THUS, THERE are regulations by law that you need to abide by to avoid any troubles. The idea is to live in total freedom without worrying about any kind of legal hassle and making money through an RV lifestyle. It's never wise to dive into something without doing enough research on it. A motorhome life has plenty of adventures and surprises in store for you. However, there are certain limitations that you need to adjust to. You need to follow certain rules as defined by the state you are in—RV parking rules, traffic and road laws, and storage laws.

As long as you are aware of all the legalities and you adhere to them, an RV life is a dream come true. The more sorted you are in your day-to-day life, the easier it will be for you to work and make your ends meet. So, switching to an RV life comes with a lot of responsibility. You can't just do whatever you feel like. Before you even purchase an RV, do some thorough research on its usage. You can't simply park your motorhome anywhere, not even in your own backyard! The rules and ordinances vary from state to state. For instance, you can park your RV in your backyard in most rural precincts of Ohio and the other such areas of the United States, while it's restricted in the city of Dayton.

RV Parking Rules to Abide by

According to the federal statutes, you are allowed to park up to five vehicles on your premises, and one of them can be an RV. However, your RV should not be linked to services like water, electricity, or gas. There are other specifications like your RV should not be more than 30 feet in length; it should be kept functional and have an updated license. And, if you reside in an area that is ruled by a homeowner's association (HOA), you may have to abide by some additional laws.

While you may park your RV for a night or so on some streets, most cities do not let you park like that. Also, there are areas that are reserved for RVs by the state, but it's not so easy to find space for your vehicle. Thus, buying an RV is not the only part you have to deal with. You also need to be aware of the parking limitations and the state rules.

What about living in your RV in your own backyard or property premises? You may be allowed to live in your RV while your house is being renovated or fumigated. Typically, the United States Department of Housing and Urban Development does not permit you to live in an RV even in your own backyard because it's not considered a permanent dwelling. According to the federal government laws, RVs are not supposed to be used for any other purpose other than the purpose of travel, camping, and recreation.

It may sound strange, but if you live in an RV on your premises or on your friend's property, you will face the same legal troubles. Not just that, but even your friend or family member may get into a legal hassle because of you parking in their space.

Thus, you should avoid making your home in an RV on any residential premises. You have two options to live in your motorhome legally—you need to rent a space at a registered RV park. That way, you will also have access to water, electricity, and other utilities. The other way to live in your RV is by traveling in your RV. As you cruise through the country in your RV, you can make your home temporarily at RV parks, campsites, and other establishments. Since you will not be residing in a place for a prolonged period of time, there shouldn't be a legal problem.

If your RV is bigger than the usual size, you should ensure that you have a special driver's license for you to explore the country extensively or you may land in trouble. So yes, the size of your RV matters. Although you can have an RV with a maximum height of 14' as directed by most states, restrictions of 13'6" are usual. Similarly, the length of your motorhome is mostly limited to 45'; however, motorhomes that come with a separate trailer are typically limited to a length of 50' to 65'.

In addition, almost all the states require you to have a breakaway switch and safety chain for your RV's safety. You should also know that certain states like Massachusetts and Maryland restrict the travel of LP gas between certain points, particularly between tunneled highways. So, you might have to find other routes if your vehicle uses LP for any devices.

RV STORAGE LAWS

Another matter to consider is long-term RV storage—you may keep your RV on your own property in some states, but you never know, homeowners' associations or some communities might have objections. You may be asked to arrange for a permanent space for your RV when it's not in use. If you don't adhere to the parking rules for an RV, it may result in a heavy penalty or even the loss of driving privileges.

To ensure a smooth and enjoyable RV life, you must plan your RV parking and storage in advance. These laws and ordinances are practiced for your own safety and also for the security of other drivers and passengers on the roadways.

Abiding by RV rules will help you live without fear or stress. You will be able to work comfortably and generate a constant flow of cash in your pocket while exploring various beautiful places. You can choose to do anything from camp hosting to launching your own business without breaking any RV laws.

Making Money Without Breaking the Laws

You can live peacefully while following your dream of living in an RV. There are many ways to earn an income along with your adventures while also following all state regulations.

Seasonal Jobs That Offer Parking Space for Your RV

In addition to the income you make, there are seasonal jobs offered by the National Park Service and its Concessionaires that you can take up. You can work at national parks at the lodges, campgrounds, and restaurants; take up jobs like camp hosting, housekeeping, maintenance, and sanitary work. And, since some of the largest parks have campgrounds exclusively for their staff, it's ideal for an RV life.

It's a good opportunity to stay in one place for at least some time and not be worried about parking your RV. You get to work and make money, even though it's temporary, meet different people, and make wonderful memories. Yes, you should be careful and understand that certain camp host positions demand a lot of your time in exchange for a free camping space.

More seasonal work that offers RV parks for your stay are jobs at ski resorts, museums, theme parks, and other such attractions. The best part is that you get a safe place to sojourn and garner so many new experiences.

Work at Farms

You can also work at farms as a temporary harvest worker and roll in quite a few dollars quickly. For instance, the sugar beet harvest pays really well. Although the job is hard and the days can be long, it's a great experience. Picking Jobs is a site worth checking out for other seasonal harvesting jobs anywhere in the country.

Work at Oil Fields

Another job that's hard but pays really well is working at the gates of energy companies at the secluded oil fields of the country. They typically employ two RVers to work for 12 hours straight. You can also try and take up jobs like pipeline construction or inspection offered by energy companies that require you to travel in RVs while working. So, it can be an excellent combination for you, as there's no possibility of getting into any kind of legal problem in terms of your vehicle.

Work at Medical Facilities

If you are a medical professional, you can be hired as temporary radiologists, nurses, and other medical specialists to take advantage of a traveling lifestyle and make money at the same time. You get to visit several medical facilities where your specialized skills are required for a period of time.

Work at Job Sites

Additionally, you can offer your services in the building trades—you can take up any job that suits your qualification and experience—technician, engineer, electrician, or laborer. You work till the project is finished, and once it's done, you can travel, and then again move to a new place and begin making money.

So, there are quite a lot of seasonal work options that suit your RV lifestyle. They pay you well and you don't have to be bothered about any regulations. All you need to focus on is savoring each new experience and enjoying the freedom.

AFTERWORD

Now that you have read the book and have learned the ways to make money while living in an RV, you should get down to implementing the strategies and kick-start your dream life. Nothing is too good to be true. You are the author of your own life. It's time you take charge of it and set out to do the things that you are meant to do. Everybody is different. Not everybody has the same passions and dreams; thus, not everybody is supposed to do the same thing or run after the same paycheck. You are different, so accept it and take action toward creating a life that you have been longing to live. Don't wait for things to happen on their own or for your fate to change. No, it's never going to happen. It's you who has to make a decision today—to quit your job, come out of the corporate slavery, and breathe in fresh air.

Nothing in life is a bed of roses. You have to work hard at everything you put your mind to—be it an RV life, travel, or creating passive income streams. But you need to make up your mind to do it. As long as you are honest about your vision and goals in life, you can achieve anything. Even if you need to learn a few new skills or network with different people, you should not shy away from broadening your horizons. There's no dearth of freelance work in today's digital age when anyone can work from anywhere and generate a steady income. All you need to do is be aware and do your research. The trend of the laptop life-style is on a rise and it's for the good of everyone. So, take advantage of that and learn how to adapt to the changing trend and make it work for you in a sustainable way.

You should also change your mindset and move away from things that have little or no value. Don't be lured by great shopping discounts and hoard stuff in your house that might not be of any use to you later. Don't envy other people's flashy lifestyle. Don't do things to make an impression or to feel part of the crowd. Be your own self by pursuing things that make you happy. Set your priorities right. Write down your short and long-term goals. Find ways to fulfill them. If you want to live in an RV and enjoy the freedom of working from anywhere, find out what you need to do to be able to live that way.

Perhaps you need to choose minimalism, simplicity, and discipline to reach your goals. Passive income that everybody dreams of isn't a game of trial and error but of research, planning, building the right strategies, and consistent work. Nothing great is built in a day. Things evolve and begin to take shape over a period of time. If you start a food business in your RV, it's going to take some time to be popular and generate some revenue for you.

Passive income isn't a myth for sure. It's time you leave the misconceptions about it behind and begin to understand its benefits and long-term impact on your life. You should have some sort of passive earnings to support your dreams of travel and living without a permanent job or house. Although passive income is not something you can create in a short span of time, it's definitely something that grows exponentially later as you continue to maintain it. As a digital nomad, you should always be looking out for different income streams by monetizing your skills and talents.

Now that you have learned about so many ways to make money from an RV, you should be able to pick and choose the ones that suit your experience, qualifications, and lifestyle. It's also important to adjust to the digital nomad way of life and learn to live with the limitations. You may not feel super productive all the time or able to deliver your client's work in a jiffy. So, be well prepared for such creative or mental blocks. Plan your work environment in advance, keep yourself motivated by working in the right kind of a setting, and avoid distractions.

Always remind yourself of the benefits of life on wheels. Look for RV work opportunities that pay you well, give you free parking spaces, safety, and the ability to explore new places.

An RV life has its own share of challenges, but it gives you the freedom and flexibility to live each day as you like. You can make a decent income, which is not just enough to fill your belly, but to fill your plate with some nice dessert, too!

If you found the book informative, please leave a review on Amazon. Enjoy RVing!

You have reached the end of this book!

I hope you enjoyed it as much as I enjoyed writing it.

I would love it if you would share your opinion with others,
leaving a review!

Every single review is very important to me, because they allow me to:

Find out what's missing in my book, updating it for my reader
&
Continue my writing activity

TO BRING YOU NEW HIGH QUALITY CONTENT!

Other people like you and me might decide to start a revolution in their lives by following this fantastic lifestyle.

Thank You and I Wish You a Great Start to Your RV Adventure Around the World!

DON'T MISS YOUR GIFT!

For You who read this book to *Begin a Brand-New RV Adventure,*

WE ARE GIVING AWAY

the second book in the *RV LIFE* collection:

"RV Passive Income Guide"

Learn how to <u>Generate Passive Income</u> so you can live

365 Days a Year in Your RV
Without Having to Think about Finances!

Frame this QR with your smartphone to
Download it FOR FREE!

HAVE A GOOD READ!

REFERENCES

Anderson, M. (2021, April 2). So, you're thinking of living the RV life. Lonely Planet. https://www.lonelyplanet.com/articles/living-in-an-rv

Birken, E. G. (2021, December 2). Top Passive Income Ideas. Forbes Advisor. https://www.forbes.com/advisor/investing/passive-income-ideas/

Brand, N. (2018). Man picking foods on trays [Online Image]. https://unsplash.com/photos/kbcqR60zWeo

Chaudhry, S. (2021). Silhouette of three men standing near white van [Online Image]. https://unsplash.com/photos/7vyTHevoeJM

Distel, A. (2019). Person holding black iPhone displaying stock exchange [Online Image]. https://unsplash.com/photos/nGc5RT2HmF0

Doyle, A. (2020, November 18). Preparing for and Landing a Babysitting Job. The Balance Careers. https://www.thebalancecareers.com/babysitting-jobs-2062240

Dumlao, N. (2018). Laptop on woman lap [Online Image]. https://unsplash.com/photos/Xe7WJc6ZV5k

Esajian, P. (2015, January 15). 9 Passive Income Myths Busted. Fortune-Builders. https://www.fortunebuilders.com/9-passive-income-myths-busted/

French, S. (2020, December 2). Renting Out Your RV: The Pandemic Side Hustle. NerdWallet. https://www.nerdwallet.com/article/travel/why-renting-out-your-rv-has-become-a-lucrative-pandemic-side-hustle

Galea, L. (2021, November 3). 10 Companies That Let You Teach English Online Without a Degree. www.international tefl academy.com. https://www.internationalteflacademy.com/blog/5-companies-that-let-you-teach-english-online-without-a-degree

Gradert, K. (2020). White car on road during daytime [Online Image]. https://unsplash.com/photos/Jbe2bX-fTmg

Guillaume, A. (2020). Green trees on brown sand near a body of water during daytime [Online Image]. https://unsplash.com/photos/KitOeE0vXzI

Is It Legal to Live in a Camper in Your Backyard? (2020, January 8). Suhre & Associates, LLC. https://suhrelawdayton.com/blog/is-it-legal-to-live-in-a-camper-in-your-backyard/

Jessica. (2021, September 11). What it's Like to be an Amazon Camper-Force Employee. Exploring the Local Life. https://www.exploringthelocallife.com/what-its-like-to-be-an-amazon-camperforce-employee/

Levin, H. (2021, December 13). How to Prepare for Full-Time RV Living: Tips & Checklist. Money Crashers. https://www.moneycrashers.com/prepare-living-rv-full-time-tips-checklist/

Lillico, T. (2017). Pink, white, and orange blanket inside tent near body of water [Online Image]. https://unsplash.com/photos/PRU6-3v8n7I

Lisbin, T. (2017). Parked van near mountain [Online Image]. https://unsplash.com/photos/tQeTKUnI4Ow

Mallorca, T. (2019). White and red wooden house beside gray framed magnifying glass [Online Image]. https://unsplash.com/photos/NpTb-VOkkom8

May, D. (2020, January 31). 8 Common Money Myths Debunked. Antidote. https://antidote.substack.com/p/8-common-money-myths-debunked

McCutcheon, S. (2018a). Person holding fan of U.S. dollars banknote [Online Image]. https://unsplash.com/photos/rItGZ4vquWk

McCutcheon, S. (2018b). Focus photography of a person counting dollar banknotes [Online Image]. https://unsplash.com/photos/-8a5eJ1-mmQ

Meurisse, M. (2017). Person lying on a couch with a body of water view at dusk [Online Image]. https://unsplash.com/photos/flWsg878m_I

Meyer, M. (2018). People sitting down near a table with assorted laptop computers [Online Image]. https://unsplash.com/photos/SYTO3xs06fU

Michael. (2020, January 27). How to Become a Digital Nomad in 2021, Step-by-Step | Detailed Guide. Hobo with a Laptop. https://hobowith-alaptop.com/become-digital-nomad

Michelle, V. S. (2020). Green plant in clear glass vase [Online Image]. https://unsplash.com/photos/ZVprbBmT8QA

Montgomery, C. (2020). Macbook pro displaying a group of people [Online Image]. https://unsplash.com/photos/smgTvepind4

Reichmuth, D. (2016). Yellow Volkswagen van on road [Online Image]. https://unsplash.com/photos/A5rCN8626Ck

Royal, J. (2022, January 1). 14 Passive Income Ideas To Help You Make Money In 2021. Bankrate. https://www.bankrate.com/investing/passive-income-ideas/

RV Laws to Consider | RV Parking, Storage & Traffic Laws | KOA Camping Blog. (n.d.). Koa.com. https://koa.com/blog/the-beginners-guide-to-buying-an-rv-laws-and-other-items/

Talk, R. (2020). Life on roads. RVing in Grand Canyon National Park. [Online Image]. https://unsplash.com/photos/Fk5cBS4BUvQ

Trabue, A. (2020, May 24). 30 Ways To Make Money While Full-Time RVing. RV MILES. https://rvmiles.com/30-ways-to-make-money-while-full-time-rving/

Tullius, T. (2017). White minivan parked near trees in the daytime [Online Image]. https://unsplash.com/photos/HxEAZylvr2U

Tysiak, I. (2018). Black scientific calculator, orange, and notebook on table [Online Image]. https://unsplash.com/photos/kRaH720CCRE

Ventur, E. (2021). Woman in black long sleeve shirt covering her face with her hands [Online Image]. https://unsplash.com/photos/bmJAXAz6ads

Whelen, P. (2021). White and blue tram on road during daytime [Online Image]. https://unsplash.com/photos/Q3MXOdErj04

Widmer, B. (2019, April 8). The Pros & Cons of Living In An RV. Mapping Megan. https://www.mappingmegan.com/pros-cons-of-living-in-an-rv/

Made in the USA
Columbia, SC
01 May 2022

59788566R00067